The series editors:

Adrian Beard is Head of English at Gosforth High School in Newcastle upon Tyne and a chief examiner for A Level English Literature. He has written and lectured extensively on the subjects of literature and language. His publications include *Texts and Contexts* (Routledge).

Angela Goddard is Senior Lecturer in Language at the Centre for Human Communication, Manchester Metropolitan University and was Chief Moderator for English Language A Level Project Research for the Northern Examination and Assessment Board (NEAB) from 1983 to 1995. She is now Chair of Examiners for A Level English Language. Her publications include *Researching Language* (2nd edn, Heinemann 2000).

Core textbook:

Working with Texts: A core introduction to language analysis (2nd edn, 2001)
Ronald Carter, Angela Goddard, Danuta Reah, Keith Sanger, Maggie Bowring

Satellite titles:

Language and Gender
Angela Goddard and Lesley Meân Patterson

The Language of Advertising: Written texts (2nd edn)
Angela Goddard

The Language of Conversation
Francesca Pridham

The Language of Drama
Keith Sanger

The Language of Fiction
Keith Sanger

The Language of Humour
Alison Ross

The Language of ICT: Information and communication technology
Tim Shortis

The Language of Magazines
Linda McLoughlin

The Language of Newspapers (2nd edn)
Danuta Reah

The Language of Poetry
John McRae

The Language of Politics
Adrian Beard

The Language of Speech and Writing
Sandra Cornbleet and Ronald Carter

The Language of Sport
Adrian Beard

The Language of Television
Jill Marshall and Angela Werndly

Inter te**X**t

The Language of Magazines

'Clear and detailed, the book brings theory alive as it encourages students to investigate magazines, pointing them to the relevant and interesting areas.'

Francesca Pridham, *Winstanley College, Wigan, Lancashire*

'This excellent book is the first ever to focus exclusively on the language of magazines. Detailed and full of examples, it is nevertheless highly accessible and is sure to prove popular with students.'

Dr Mary Talbot, *School of Arts, Design and Media, University of Sunderland*

This accessible satellite textbook in the Routledge INTERTEXT series is unique in offering students hands-on practical experience of textual analysis focused on magazines. Written in a clear, user-friendly style by an experienced teacher, it combines practical activities with texts, followed by commentaries and suggestions for further reading. It can be used individually or in conjunction with the series core textbook, *Working with Texts: A core book for language analysis*.

Aimed at A-Level and beginning undergraduate students, *The Language of Magazines*:

- shows how linguistic techniques such as puns and presuppositions are used by magazines to capture our attention
- examines how image and text combine to produce meaning
- discusses how ideological messages are conveyed
- analyses how gender is constructed through language
- looks at how magazines relate to culture
- explores a wide variety of magazines, including *Cosmopolitan*, *Men's Health*, *Bliss*, *Diva*, *FHM*, *Sugar* and *Viz*

Linda McLoughlin is a part-time lecturer in English Language at Edge Hill College, Ormskirk, Lancashire. She has designed and taught BA and MA courses in English Language, specialising in language and gender.

The Intertext series

◎ Why does the phrase 'spinning a yarn' refer both to using language and making cloth?

◎ What might a piece of literary writing have in common with an advert or a note from the milkman?

◎ What aspects of language are important to understand when analysing texts?

The Routledge INTERTEXT series aims to develop reader's understanding of how texts work. It does this by showing some of the designs and patterns in the language from which they are made, by placing texts within the context in which they occur, and by exploring relationships between them.

The series consists of a foundation text, *Working with Texts: A core introduction to language analysis*, which looks at language aspects essential for the analysis of texts, and a range of satellite titles. These apply aspects of language to a particular topic area in more detail. They complement the core text and can also be used alone, providing the user has the foundation skills furnished by the core text.

Benefits of using this series:

◎ **Multi-disciplinary** – provides a foundation for the analysis of texts, supporting students who want to achieve a detailed focus on language.

◎ **Accessible** – no previous knowledge of language analysis is assumed, just an interest in language use.

◎ **Student-friendly** – contains activities relating to texts studied, commentaries after activities, highlighted key terms, suggestions for further reading and an index of terms.

◎ **Interactive** – offers a range of task-based activities both for class use and self study.

◎ **Tried and tested** – written by a team of respected teachers and practitioners whose ideas and activities have been trialled independently.

The Language of Magazines

- Linda McLoughlin

LONDON AND NEW YORK

First published 2000
by Routledge
11 New Fetter Lane, London EC4P 4EE

Simultaneously published in the USA
and Canada
by Routledge
29 West 35th Street, New York, NY 10001

Reprinted 2002

Routledge is an imprint of the Taylor & Francis Group

© 2000 Linda McLoughlin

Typeset in Stone Sans/Stone Serif

Printed and bound in Great Britain by
TJ International Ltd, Padstow, Cornwall

British Library Cataloguing in Publication Data
A catalogue record for this book is
available from the British Library

Library of Congress Cataloging in Publication Data
McLoughlin, Linda, 1957–
   The language of magazines / Linda
   McLoughlin.
   p. cm. – (Intertext)
   Includes bibliographical references
   and index.
   ISBN 0–415–21424–6 (alk. paper)
   1. Mass media and
   language.   2. Periodicals.   3. Discourse
   analysis.   I. Title.   II. Intertext
   (London, England)

P96.L34 M367 2000
302.23'01'4–dc21
                                    99-048842

contents

Unit five: Who am I?: the relationship between the text producer and interpreter

Unit six: The discourse of magazines

Unit seven: Representations of women and men: constructing femininity, masculinity and sexuality

acknowledgements

I would like to thank Joy Bowes for reading and commenting on units two and five. Thanks also to Angela Goddard for her invaluable editorial support and advice. Special thanks are due to Mary Talbot whose work in this field has been a tremendous influence on my own.

The following illustrations and texts have been reprinted by courtesy of their copyright holders:

Bella Front cover, Reader's tip, Horoscope: H. Bauer Publishing Limited.
Bliss 'Will we end up gay?', 'All made up', 'The ultimate sex checklist' and Libra horoscope: Emap Elan Ltd.
Cosmopolitan 'From the Editor', Reader's Letter (photo: Fritz Kok), 'The crazy, *crazy* world of international beauty queens' (photos: Eric Morley, Miss World (Jersey) Ltd), 'Brand Nude' (photos: Robert Fairer/Chris Moore), Horoscope (photos: All Action/Gettyone Stone), 'Get Eurosavvy!' (photos: Rex Features), 'A man for all reasons': © The National Magazine Company.
Diva cover: copyright Em Fitzgerald/*Diva*.
FHM Front cover, 'Editor's Letter', Readers' Letters, 'Pulse' and *FHM Bionic* 'The icy plunge': Emap Metro Ltd.
GQ Active 'Bread winners': Simon Mills © *GQ Active*/The Condé Nast Publications Ltd.
J-17 Snog Guide: Emap Elan Ltd.
Sugar 'Don't become a mum by mistake': Attic Futura.
Tatler Front cover, 'Editor's Letter' and 'The importance of being a posh footballer': David Tama (photo)/Jane Proctor/Olivia Stewart Liberty © *Tatler*/The Condé Nast Publications Ltd.
Viz Readers' letters: House of Viz/John Brown Publishing 1999.

The publishers have made every effort to contact copyright holders, although this has not been possible in all cases. The publishers would be grateful to hear from any copyright holder who is not here acknowledged and will undertake to rectify any errors or omissions in future editions of this book.

list of main texts

Text: **Collage of titles**
Minx, Tatler, More!, GQ Active, Cosmopolitan, Men's Health, FHM, Diva, Bella

Text: **Front covers**
Tatler, June 1999
Men's Health, July/August 1998
FHM, February 2000
Bella, 25 August 1998
Diva, May 1999

Text: **The importance of being a posh footballer**
Tatler, June 1999

Text: **The crazy, *crazy* world of international beauty queens**
Cosmopolitan, September 1998

Text: **'We're an item'**
Men's Health, July/August 1998

Text: **It's a man's world**
Men's Health, July/August 1998

Text: **Next month in Men's Health**
Men's Health, July/August 1998

Text: **Horoscopes**
Bella, 25 August 1998
Bliss, May 1998
Cosmopolitan, September 1998
More!, 22 November–5 December 1995

Text: **Readers' letters**
The naked truth (*Cosmopolitan*, September 1998)
No more tears (*Bella*, 25 August 1998)

Letter of the month (*Men's Health*, July/August 1998)
All made-up (*Bliss*, May 1998)
Dannii, part one (*FHM*, February 2000)
Top Tip, Mr. Teats and Smiles better? D. Smoog (*Viz* issue 96)

Text: **The problem page**
Will we end up gay? (*Bliss*, July 1996)

Text: **Reader's true story**
Don't become a mum by mistake (*Sugar*, December 1997)

Text: **Editors' letters**
Cosmopolitan, September 1998
FHM, February 2000

Text: **Get Eurosavvy!**
Cosmopolitan, September 1998

Text: **The icy plunge**
FHM Bionic, Winter/Spring 2000

Text: **Knit a jumper for your dog**
The Girl's Own Paper, January 1935

Text: **Snog Guide**
J-17, September 1997

Text: **Pulse**
FHM, February 1997

Text: **Brand nude**
Cosmopolitan, September 1998

introduction

Magazines are an immensely popular cultural form as can be seen from the circulation figures of two popular monthly magazines:

Cosmopolitan   441,536
FHM   504,959
(Willings Press Guide 1998)

It's difficult to estimate the precise numbers of readers of magazines since they are often handed on by the purchaser to be read by family and friends. Added to this is the opportunity to browse magazines in public places such as doctors' waiting rooms which makes it even more difficult to accurately assess the circulation figures, but unlike newspapers, which become out of date the day after publication, magazines have a relatively long shelf-life.

Despite their popularity a prevailing view is that magazines are a low brow form of entertainment. Magazines do not have to be read from cover to cover but can be dipped into, their format makes them easy to pick up and put down again. It is this reason which has been used to explain the popularity of magazines among women. The association of magazines with women has been linked to their domestic role, but not necessarily one which presents women as 'tied to the kitchen sink.' Instead there is said to be a subversive potential which offers women an opportunity to take time off from domestic chores and have some time to themselves. This is somewhat outdated now in view of the number of women who work outside the home. There is also a growing market of magazines aimed at men, some of which are outstripping the sales of women's magazines.

There are many other areas of social life which have copied the magazine's format. This has been introduced into a wide range of **genres** (genre is another word for text-type), for example, public health leaflets; so you might like to apply the suggestions in this book to these other forms. Often serious subjects like AIDs can be dealt with in this user-friendly way. A particular type of daytime television is known as the magazine programme, e.g. *Richard and Judy*. This is partly due to the content, which is similar to that found in magazines with topics such as beauty, cookery, fashion and an interest in the lives of celebrities. There has also been the adoption of a 'how to' genre which shows TV viewers a range of activities from 'how to copy the latest catwalk looks' to 'how to get and keep a toyboy'.

The easy-to-read format of magazines does not mean that they are not carefully crafted. This book will introduce readers to the notion that magazines require us to interact with them in complex ways. Magazines have their own particular ethos and ideologies but they can also reflect and construct cultural values. In order for the texts to work they must draw on the readers' knowledge of language. It is the language of magazines that will be the central focus of this book.

Unit one

What is a magazine?

Aim of this unit

The aim of unit one is to explain what magazines are and to consider the types of magazines which are currently available. The production process will also be examined to illustrate that there is a whole range of people involved in this, from market researchers to copywriters.

What is a magazine?

Magazines are such a popular and familiar form that it may seem strange even to ask this question. Nevertheless let's see what the dictionary says:

> **magazine** n. 1. a periodic paperback
> publication containing articles, fiction,
> photographs, etc.
>
> *The Collins Concise Dictionary*

The first point to note is the reference to frequency. Magazines are issued at regular intervals either weekly, fortnightly, monthly or quarterly. The next reference is to the material form of magazines. *Paperback* is a term now used to refer to a type of book rather than a magazine, but you may know older people who refer to magazines as books. The quality of the material of today's magazines can vary; weekly publications are made of a cheaper quality paper whereas monthly magazines are higher quality, often using glossy paper. The quality of the paper can have an effect on the **connotations** which the magazine conveys. Connotations are the associations which a word or concept has for the reader, for example, glossy paper connotes sophistication and glamour. These are the magazines which are likely to be found adorning coffee tables, the type that people like to show off. The last reference in our definition concerns the content of magazines - articles, fiction and photographs – which relates to the original meaning of the word *magazine*: 'storehouse of information'. This **heterogeneity** (a composition of unrelated parts) is perhaps the magazine's most obvious feature. Although the format has changed over the years these three items are a staple of many magazines. Some magazines aimed at young women used to combine fiction and photographs which produced the photostory. This particular form is now outdated but illustrates the point that the format of magazines changes with the times.

What types of magazines are there?

A glance at the newsagents shelves shows that the magazine genre covers a broad spectrum: there are special interest magazines dealing with topics like computing, DIY, household crafts and music, to name just a few, and the language of these magazines will reflect their specialist nature. There are also what are referred to as 'centre of interest' magazines which are aimed at a much wider audience. Most recently the magazine format has been incorporated into Sunday newspaper supplements. Supermarkets are also producing their own 'in-house' magazines. Added to this list is a new type of magazine to be found on the Internet, referred to as the e-zine.

In order to provide a focus, it is the centre of interest magazine which consumers consciously select and purchase which will be the topic of this textbook.

Who produces magazines?

Often, apparent rival magazines may be produced by the same publisher. Two of the major publishers in the UK are Emap Elan Limited, who publish a number of magazines including *Just Seventeen, It's Bliss, Minx* and *More!*, and IPC Magazines, who publish *Mizz* and *Sugar.* The

Text : Credit Listing

COSMOPOLITAN

EDITOR
Mandi Norwood
DEPUTY EDITOR Louise Atkinson MANAGING EDITOR Carol Bronze
FEATURES EDITOR Leah Hardy NEWS EDITOR Anna Moore
CONTRIBUTING EDITOR Sarah Kennedy FEATURES WRITER Sasha Slater
EDITOR'S PA Rowena Kenyon

DESIGN
ART DIRECTOR Ellen Erickson
DEPUTY ART DIRECTOR Garry Mears
SENIOR DESIGNERS Louisa McCabe Emma Kirkham
JUNIOR DESIGNER Emma Homan
PICTURE EDITOR Marsha Arnold PICTURE ASSISTANT Hannah Hanson

EDITORIAL PRODUCTION
CHIEF SUB EDITOR/PRODUCTION EDITOR Sarah Giles
DEPUTY CHIEF SUB EDITOR/PRODUCTION EDITOR Helen Placito
SENIOR SUB EDITOR Louise Ford
SUB EDITOR Iain Reid JUNIOR SUB EDITOR Hannah Ebelthite

FASHION
FASHION DIRECTOR Bryony Toogood
FASHION EDITOR Jane Gill
FASHION & BEAUTY FEATURES WRITER Catherine Baudrand
FASHION ASSISTANT Catherine McCormack
JUNIOR FASHION ASSISTANT Sarah Bennie

HEALTH & BEAUTY
HEALTH & BEAUTY DIRECTOR Jan Masters
HEALTH & BEAUTY EDITOR Laura Bacharach
HEALTH & BEAUTY ASSISTANT Camilla Kay

READER AFFAIRS AND EVENTS MANAGER
Louise George

CONTRIBUTING EDITORS
Wendy Bristow Lucy Broadbent Caroline Knapp Anna Maxted
Ros Miles Kate Thornton

PUBLISHING DIRECTOR
Liz Kershaw
PUBLISHING DIRECTOR'S PA Helen Peasland
ADVERTISEMENT DIRECTOR Sara Stephenson
SALES DEVELOPMENT MANAGER Chris Grimes
SENIOR SALES EXECUTIVES Sarah Williams Tara Purcell
Toby Moore Natalie Konstantinovitch
ADVERTISEMENT DIRECTOR'S SECRETARY Lesley Douglas
PRODUCTION CONTROLLER Colette Curley SENIOR PRESS OFFICER Rachel Babington

THE COSMOPOLITAN SHOW
DIRECTOR OF EXHIBITIONS Stephanie Grice
DIRECTOR'S PA Belinda-Jane Hetherington
SALES MANAGER Alison Cook SENIOR SALES EXECUTIVE Tamsin Walker
SALES EXECUTIVES Anita Mills Jo Restall SHOW MANAGER Neil Levene
PROMOTIONS & MARKETING MANAGER Claudia Russell
SHOW EXECUTIVES Katie Norton Emma Williams
SALES TEAM SECRETARY Sarah Richards EXHIBITION SECRETARY Louise Phelps

DIRECTOR OF CORPORATE BUSINESS DEVELOPMENT Duncan Edwards
DIRECTOR OF CENTRAL SALES AND PROMOTIONS Tim Lucas
DIRECTOR OF PROMOTIONS Jennifer Sharp
DIRECTOR OF CLASSIFIED SALES Liz Griffiths
REGIONAL SALES DIRECTOR Patrick Taylor
DIRECTOR OF INTERNATIONAL SALES Alex Riha
DIRECTOR OF COMMUNICATIONS Eileen Wise
MANAGER, MARKETING STRATEGY Sue Coffin

GROUP GENERAL MANAGER Brian Wallis
GROUP MANUFACTURING DIRECTOR Alice Symonds
HEAD OF INFORMATION TECHNOLOGY Andrew Tunley
HEAD OF CIRCULATION Martin Granby
DIRECTOR OF NATIONAL MAGAZINE ENTERPRISES Anne Melbourne
LIBRARY AND SYNDICATION Susanna van Langenberg
DIRECTOR OF SUBSCRIPTIONS MARKETING Joan Scanlon

INTERNATIONAL EDITIONS
INTERNATIONAL EDITOR-IN-CHIEF Helen Gurley Brown
EXECUTIVE DIRECTOR INTERNATIONAL EDITIONS Kim St. Clair Bodden
EDITOR, ARGENTINA Sylvia do Pico AUSTRALIA Kate Mahon
BRAZIL Marcia Villela Neder CZECH REPUBLIC Anastazie Kudrnova
FRANCE Anne Chabrol GERMANY Lisa Feldmann
GREECE Sophia Ganiatsou HOLLAND Rieja van Aart
HONG KONG Ruqiyah Law Kam Ying HUNGARY Anita Pocsik
INDIA Simran Bhargava INDONESIA Sari Narulita JAPAN Haruka Noda
LATIN AMERICA Sara Maria Castany PHILIPPINES Myrza Sison
POLAND Grazyna Olbrych PORTUGAL Margarida Pinto Correia
RUSSIA Elena Myasnikova Ellen Verbeek SOUTH AFRICA Vanessa Raphaely
SPAIN Sarah Glattstein Franco TAIWAN Min Chun Chang
THAILAND Kaysinee Suthavarangkul TURKEY Leyla Melek US Bonnie Fuller

MANAGING DIRECTOR OF THE NATIONAL MAGAZINE COMPANY
Terry Mansfield

production process includes a range of people engaged in a variety of activities. To gain some idea of the types of activity take a look at Text: Credit listing taken from *Cosmopolitan*. How many people are listed and what type of work is involved? You might like to compare this with the credit listing of another magazine.

It will become apparent that although a page from a magazine may appear to be the product of a single author it is more than likely that several people will be involved before the page takes its final shape. It is for this reason that the term 'text producer' rather than 'writer' is a more accurate description and one which will be used throughout this book.

Extension

Meaning is culture specific. Many magazines are produced in or distributed to numerous countries overseas. According to Winship (1992) there has been a 'European invasion' of magazines within the British Isles. For example, *Best* and *Bella* are owned by German publishers Gruner & Jahr and Bauer respectively and *Hello!* by the Spanish company Hola, SA. A worthwhile project could be to examine the differences between British magazines and their foreign counterparts.

Unit two

The wrapping
Front covers

Aim of this unit

This unit will focus on the strategies adopted by text producers in order to attract our attention. The front cover is the magazine's most important advertisement but it also serves to label its possessor. The ideal-reader images offered by a selection of magazines will also be examined.

'A magazine's front-cover image and coverlines are persuasive selling tools. They motivate readers – confronted with shelves of front covers competing for their attention – to buy our magazine rather than another.' This quote from the editor's letter of *Tatler* acknowledges the vast competition which text producers face. It is little wonder then that they go to great lengths in order to make their particular magazine jump out at us from the shelves. It is through tricks of language that this is chiefly achieved, but visual images, layout and graphology also play their part. The cover of the magazine helps us to distinguish one magazine from another and although they are constantly changing in order to create variety and to keep up-to-date, they retain sufficient features to mark out their own identity.

Ideal-reader images

McCracken (1996) notes 'the cover serves to label not only the magazine but the consumer who possesses it'. What she is referring to is the way in

5

which text producers position readers and shape the reading process. The techniques used in order to achieve this will be discussed more fully in unit five but the front cover has a role in shaping the different expectations which readers have on purchasing and consuming the magazine. Readers are invited to join communities with distinct cultural identities.

What's in a name?: magazine titles

The title of the magazine plays a large part in shaping the reader's expectations. It is always written in large letters and is a shorthand way of conjuring up particular associations in the reader's mind. An analogy can be made with the brand names of products which Goddard (1998: 80) refers to as 'little concentrated capsules of meaning'.

Activity

Look at Text: Collage of titles. What information about the magazine is suggested by the title? A dictionary may be helpful for this activity.

Commentary

Some magazine titles are cryptic, for example *FHM* (for him magazine) and *GQ* (Gentlemen's Quarterly) both mean that readers have to work out what the acronyms stand for. On the other hand, some titles are information giving, e.g. *Men's Health* tells us what the magazine is about. However, 'health' has a rather expanded meaning which covers topics ranging from sex to fashion.

Titles can signify a particular character type, e.g. *Minx*. If you consult a dictionary you will see that this term could be used as an insult: 'bold flirtatious or scheming woman'. However, this is the opposite of what usually happens to words when associated with women. Schultz (1975) found that over time, words which might have began with neutral connotations undergo a process of **pejoration** (take on negative associations). 'Minx' has actually acquired positive connotations, particularly in relation to the young women who form the target age group of the magazine. This is an example of **amelioration** (when a word with negative connotations is invested with positive meaning). *Diva* has come to mean 'Prima Dona'; but its Latin meaning,: 'goddess', is possibly the association which the magazine's producers are hoping to convey. The

6

Text : *Tatler* **Cover**

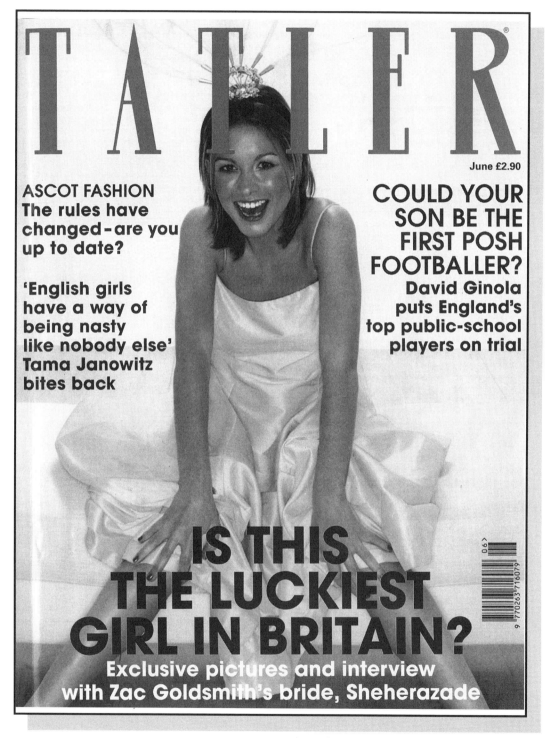

TATLER ®

June £2.90

ASCOT FASHION
The rules have
changed – are you
up to date?

'English girls
have a way of
being nasty
like nobody else'
Tama Janowitz
bites back

COULD YOUR
SON BE THE
FIRST POSH
FOOTBALLER?
David Ginola
puts England's
top public-school
players on trial

IS THIS
THE LUCKIEST
GIRL IN BRITAIN?
Exclusive pictures and interview
with Zac Goldsmith's bride, Sheherazade

8

Men's Health

JULY/AUGUST 1998 £2.90

NEW! FAT-BUSTING SPECIAL

TONS OF USEFUL STUFF

LOSE YOUR BELLY

See results in <u>2 weeks!</u>

MAKE GOOD SEX GREAT!

GET STRESS OFF YOUR BACK

10 WAYS TO SIMPLIFY YOUR LIFE
page 150

FEED YOUR MUSCLES

MAKE HER WANT YOU!

25 SELF-TESTS FOR MEN

FHM

FEBRUARY 2000 £2.90
WWW.FHM.COM

VOULEZ VOUS?
The hottest new girls in France. And they've shaved their armpits!

'I'M CONFISCATING YOUR GUN, TIMMY'
Evil kids on the rampage

HEROES ON ZIMMERS!
Meet Britain's bravest grandads

MISTER FIX-IT!
How to mend *everything* in your home

SPANK HER SILLY!
Kinky sex made simple

PLUS!
Davina McCall, speakers tested, Joseph Fiennes, coping with grief, lesbian history, Janeane Garofalo, weird coffins, Marc Anthony, nose jobs, the International Rescuer, Foo Fighters, and make your own sausages!

HONEY!
Feast your eyes on Alicia Silverstone

'HOW DARE YOU BESMIRCHIFY ME!'
We get shouted at by Don King

'STOP GRIZZLING, MAN!'
How to get dumped with dignity

9 770966 093057

contemporary meaning of *Cosmopolitan* is 'familiar with many parts of the world; sophisticated or urbane'. It is a **compound** noun (it combines two or more words into a single unit), and is derived from the Greek words *Kosmos* (the world or universe) and *polites* (citizen). No doubt the intention is to appeal to a well-travelled, sophisticated individual. *Tatler* has a reputable name as a middle-class magazine having been established in 1709. However, it is unlikely that its modern readers would be aware that *tattle* comes from middle Dutch *tatelen* meaning 'idle talk or chatter'. *Tatler* is the noun.

Magazine titles are often accompanied by slogans:

FOR girls with a lust for life (*Minx*)
Smart girls get more! (*More!*)

These slogans are deliberately ambiguous because the words *lust* and *more* have more than one meaning. For example *more* could be used as a comparative, meaning the magazine is offering more than its rivals. It could also signal *something in addition to*. The reader is left to fill in what this *something* might be. It is likely to be something positive, e.g. 'Smart girls get more from life' or, given the emphasis on sex in the contents, readers are perhaps encouraged to interpret this in a raunchy way, fitting in with the ethos of the magazine. Without doubt, a major preoccupation of today's magazines is an intensification of interest in the topic of sex. Sex can be packaged as a commodity and sold within the magazine. Even magazines aimed at young women hail this on the front covers:

Top secret sealed section (*Bliss*)

The section which is inside the centre pages has perforated edges which need to be opened before its contents can be read. This seems to add to the furtive nature of the magazine's contents and appears deliberately designed for teenagers to 'get one up' on their parents. You could look for examples in teenage magazines of the text producers addressing the reader in ways which symbolise rebellion and rejection of the ideals of the older generation.

Visual images

'The image on *Tatler's* cover represents the personality of the magazine. Each aspect is analysed, from the girl's expression to the colour of her hair

13

– everything that might make readers identify with the magazine (and part with their £2.90).' This quote, again from the editor's letter in *Tatler*, illustrates the importance of choosing the right image for the front cover. For example, the front cover of *Men's Health* shows a three-quarter body shot of a muscular male model. Presumably the reader is meant to aspire towards achieving this body type. It should be noted that this image is quite unusual for a men's magazine since a scantily clad female, the 'desired other', is the usual format. Take a look at the cover of *FHM* (on p. 10) which features a well-known actress, Alicia Silverstone. This image can be contrasted with the images of women which appear on the covers of magazines aimed at women. By way of example, on the front cover of *Bella*, the woman featured looks directly into the camera with a bemused expression on her face which is very different from that of Silverstone's quite provocative gesture and stance. These two images can be contrasted with the woman on the front cover of *Diva*, a lesbian magazine. Here the woman is striking a playful, fighting pose. The woman, unlike the other two, is not stereotypically beautiful but she exudes confidence and independence.

Activity

Collect some front covers. Describe in detail the ideal-reader images. Are these head and shoulders or full/upper body shots? Are the models looking away or directly into the camera? What do facial gestures signal? Are they smiling, pouting, aloof? Does the verbal text interact with the image? If so, how?

Layout and graphology

In our culture we learn to read from left to right, and from top to bottom of the page. It is for this reason that the prime position for important information is the top left hand corner:

LOSE YOUR
BELLY
See results in 2 weeks! (*Men's Health*)

Since the focus of this edition is on weight loss, it is easy to see why the text producer has chosen to print this in the prime position. Front covers also make good use of underlining, emboldening and a variety of font sizes, styles and colour. Unfortunately colour cannot be reproduced here but this text is quite striking – red on a white background. Other prominent colours used are black and blue. Although the model will change from issue to issue, the colours used on the cover of *Men's Health* remain characteristically red, white and blue. The graphology for the title also remains constant for easy identification. The same format is also used for the cover of the magazine's counterpart *Women's Health*.

The front cover as preview

> *Tatler's* coverlines – the teasers that attempt to describe the magazine's contents – complete the package. Again, we think about them very carefully. So I was fascinated to hear of a new strategy devised by a hugely successful American men's magazine, where the editor and team write ideal coverlines and only then commission stories to match.

Again, *Tatler's* editor is giving us an insight into the practices of magazines – the coverlines, usually, are written after the stories.

Putting words together

The text producer needs to cram a lot of information into a short space in order to tell the reader what is in store for them. This is one reason why nouns are heavily modified:

> Delicious cook-ahead stress-free feast (*Bella*)

The noun is 'feast' but look at the number of **modifiers** – 'delicious', 'cook-ahead', 'stress-free'. Modifiers are words which give more information about the noun. When modifiers come before the noun this is referred to as **pre**-modification. In listing so many pre-modifiers the text producers build up the reader's anticipation of what is coming next. Sometimes the modification comes after the head noun:

> The 10 Rules of Ex Etiquette (*Cosmopolitan*)

The head noun is 'Rules' and has the pre-modification comprising a determiner 'the' and a single modifier, '10'. 'of Ex Etiquette' is a **post-modifying** prepositional phrase. Within it the preposition 'of' is followed by another noun group 'Ex Etiquette'. 'Etiquette is the head with 'Ex' as its modifier but the prepositional phrase modifies 'Rules' (the head noun).

Having pointed out the heavy use of modification, a feature of front covers to consider is what the text producer chooses to leave out for reasons of economy. This is referred to as **elision** or **ellipsis**.

> Lose your belly
> See results in two weeks (*Men's Health*)

Presumably, *the* results the reader will see in two weeks are those of having lost their belly. The **determiner** 'the' is omitted without affecting meaning. Determiners are like adjectives, they make the meaning of nouns more specific. Examples of determiners are: 'the' (definite article), 'a' (indefinite article); 'this', 'that', 'these', 'those' (demonstratives); 'my', 'your', 'their', etc. (possessive adjectives); 'one', 'first', 'last', etc. (enumerators indicating definite quantities); 'some', 'any', 'no', 'all', etc. (indicating indefinite quantities).

Activity

Look for some examples of elision on front covers and re-write them in clear standard English. This exercise should highlight the type of words which are commonly omitted. Are these grammatical (words that signal grammatical relationships such as determiners and auxiliary verbs – 'be', 'have' and 'do') or lexical (words that have meaning such as nouns, main verbs, adjectives and adverbs)?

Creating variety: sentence types

It can prove interesting to examine the types of sentences used in magazines since this often provides an insight into the meanings made in texts. Sentences may be divided into two types: minor and major. **Minor** sentences are complete in intention but often lack a finite verb. **Finite** verbs have a tense, e.g. present or past, giving a clear idea of when something took place or whether the action has been completed. They also tell us how many are involved (singular/plural) and who the participants are:

'My ex **spied** on me from the attic' (*Bella*)

The following sentence is minor since it lacks a finite verb:

Hair **to send** him round the twist (*More!*)

You would be correct in saying that 'send' is a verb but it is **non-finite** because it is unclear when the action will be undertaken or completed. This is an example of the infinitive, the word 'to' followed by the verb. **Non-finite** verb forms do not express contrasts of tense, number, person or mood.

Turning your flat into a film set

The 'ing' participle in 'Turning' makes the verb non-finite because it is not clear when the action is to take place.

Sometimes in minor sentences the subject will be omitted:

STARTS THIS WEEK: ONLY IN BELLA
YOUR CHANCE TO CONSULT
PRINCESS
DIANA'S
PSYCHIC!

The subject of a sentence is normally the noun, noun phrase or pronoun which appears before the verb. In order to insert a subject into this sentence we would have to invent one – 'It starts this week...'; or we could rearrange the sentence – 'Your chance to consult Princess Diana's psychic starts this week.' Minor sentences appear frequently on front covers and in headers of magazines. As can be seen from this example, the term minor has nothing to do with the length or complexity of the sentence.

Activity

Divide the following into major/minor sentences:

'Aliens forced me to have sex'
LOUD AND PROUD
Asian dykes speak out
10 ways
to simplify
your life

17

Commentary

'Aliens forced me to have sex' is a major sentence because 'forced' is a finite verb ('Aliens' are the subjects and 'me' is the object).

'LOUD AND PROUD Asian dykes speak out' is also a major sentence because 'speak' is a finite verb. 'Asian dykes' are the subject. 'LOUD AND PROUD' is a noun phrase.

'10 ways to simplify your life' is a minor sentence because it lacks a finite verb. 'To simplify' is the infinitive form of the verb and is therefore non-finite.

Sentence functions

It can also be interesting to look at the functions which sentences serve to see whether the text producer prefers a particular type and if so what this might signal about the text. Sentences can be divided into four types:

- Declaratives: This type of sentence makes a statement or assertion – *All Saints get mucky*
- Imperatives: Give orders or make requests – *Get stress off your back*
- Interrogatives: Ask questions – *Feeding friends?*
- Exclamatives: These are used to express surprise, alarm or a strong opinion and are accompanied by an exclamation mark – *Nice tackle!*

Of course, these sentence types may function differently depending on the context in which the utterance takes place and also its purpose. This branch of language study is known as pragmatics. For example, 'All Saints get mucky' was categorised above as a declarative, however, if All Saints were present at the time the utterance was made it could have the force of an imperative and All Saints might well respond by getting mucky.

Activity

Categorise the sentences into the four functions:

> Do you need a second income?
> Most couples assume that both partners need to work.
> It's men v women in the sexually-sussed stakes!
> WIN a trip to Hollywood!

The headers of the *Men's Health* magazine echo the tone of the magazine's content by an abundance of short, sharp and snappy imperatives:

LOSE YOUR
BELLY
See results in 2 weeks!

FEED YOUR
MUSCLES

**MAKE GOOD
SEX GREAT!**

**MAKE HER
WANT YOU!**

GET STRESS
OFF YOUR
BACK

These are classified as major sentences although there is no overt subject. For imperatives, it is conventionally understood that the interpreter is the subject. This lack of a specified agent gives the text a sense of timelessness. The text producer, in issuing commands, is attempting to stir the reader into the action proposed. Exclamation marks are a feature of punctuation which proliferate on front covers. They can be used to convey emotion, heighten involvement and give the text a sense of immediacy which is clearly the case in the above examples. Note there are no softeners such as 'please' to reduce the force of the command which is given as if from a sergeant major, yet the reader is unlikely to take offence.

As mentioned, the front cover gives the reader a glimpse of what is to follow in the rest of the magazine. Along with the ideal image presented to readers on the front cover of *Bella* are the previews:

STARTS THIS WEEK: ONLY IN BELLA
YOUR CHANCE TO CONSULT
PRINCESS
DIANA'S
PSYCHIC!

The text producers attempt to distinguish their particular magazine from others – 'ONLY IN BELLA'. This technique continues on the page where the feature appears, a 'ticker-tape' effect repeats the phrase:

ONLY IN BELLA ONLY IN BELLA ONLY IN BELLA ONLY IN BELLA

19

The impression is of a news scoop which is available only to the readers of this particular magazine. This is an example of the lengths to which text producers will go in distinguishing their particular magazine from its rivals.

A mainstay of women's magazines is the reader's 'true' story where readers are invited to write in to the magazine and other readers are allowed a voyeuristic glimpse into their lives. Two of the articles previewed on the front cover are the real life stories of readers.

> 'MY EX SPIED ON ME
> – FROM THE ATTIC'
>
> SPECIAL REPORT
> THE NEW CULTS
> 'They brainwashed my husband – how
> I won him back'

The stories are introduced by quotations, we are to imagine, from the readers themselves which just *happen* to be the most sensational aspects of the story. Even if we accept that the stories are authentic, they are nevertheless subject to some form of editing; for example, the text producer selects which story to publish and which aspects of it to highlight. The kind of sensationalism illustrated above encourages the reader to purchase and consume the magazine since they are compelled to read on in order to discover how the woman wins back her brainwashed husband.

Problems and solutions

The next set of headings introduce another feature of magazines which is the problem/solution format. This is where the text producer anticipates that the reader is in need of advice. Unlike the stark commands of *Men's Health*, the text producer of *Bella* simulates conversation in an attempt to reduce the distance between themselves and the reader. A question is posed which is designed to raise the problem in the reader's mind:

> Feeding friends? Relax!
> Delicious cook-ahead,
> stress-free feast (*Bella*)

Notice how once the topic has been introduced this is immediately followed up by reassurance, 'Relax!', and a solution, 'Delicious cook-ahead, stress-free feast'. In this way the authority of the text producer is reduced to that of a friend giving advice.

However, some information is presented more directly:

CANCER BREAKTHROUGHS: THE FACTS YOU NEED

The text producer affects to know the reader so well she even knows what they need. Possibly, due to the seriousness of the subject, the text producer appears less concerned about sounding too authoritarian.

Tricks of language

Given the immense competition mentioned, text producers use an array of linguistic tools in order to attract our attention. The first three examples you might expect to see only in poetry:

◎ **Rhyme**

> *Catch* him, *snatch* him, make him yours.

The repetition of the word 'him' is also effective here. Repetition is a feature of **rhetoric** (the art or skill of effective communication).

◎ **Alliteration** is when the initial consonant sound is repeated in adjacent words. When this is 's', as in the first example, this is known as **sibilant** alliteration:

> **S**ix **s**imple **s**ecrets to keep you
> looking fabulous
>
> **B**oarding **b**abes
>
> **F**risky **f**ellas

◎ **Assonance** is when the same vowel sound is repeated in adjacent words.

> Fake mates

A characteristic of magazines is the vocabulary of excess to emphasise the fun and entertainment value:

21

10 Snip-*tastic* pages!
Hair special
there's *zillions* of styles to suit you!

This is also achieved by **superlatives** which are the third term in a three term system of comparison, e.g. 'good/better/best'. Superlatives offer a comparison to the highest degree:

Scrap the rest we've got the *best*

Text producers of magazines love to play around with language. Some of the cleverest ways of doing this is through **puns**:

Frisky Fellas
How to *spring* the little *lambs* (*More!*)

Nice *tackle!*
The sexiest rugby players
you've ever seen (*More!*)

Cheque mate. Marc Burford's the man
for girls who just want to have fun. (*More!*)

Some words are **polysemous** which means that they have more than one meaning. This allows text producers the scope to play around with those separate meanings. In the first example the pun is on the words 'spring' and 'lambs'. 'Spring' could mean how to trap boys or 'spring', as in the lambing season. 'Tackle' can mean a physical challenge to an opponent in sport or more recently slang for male genitalia. 'Cheque mate' is slightly different because it is a **homophone**. Homophones are words that are spelt differently but have the same sound – check/cheque. 'Check-mate' is a winning position in chess whereas 'cheque mate' is presumably a mate who supplies cheques.

Intertextuality is when reference is made to another text:

Look who's stalking!
Boys Are Us!
CURL POWER!

The first example is a well-known saying and reference to the title of a film, *Look who's Talking*. The second reminds us of a well-known toyshop, 'Toys 'R' Us' and 'Girl Power' is a modern teenage catch phrase. These references are made meaningful because of the phonological similarity between the words 'stalking/talking', 'boys/toys' and 'curl/girl'.

Idiomatic phrases are patterns of words which function as a single unit of meaning:

How's your father?
No that's my boyfriend

Snogs ahoy!

Phrases such as 'How's your father?', although well known within a culture, can present problems for those outside it since meaning cannot be worked out from the individual words. 'How's your father?' is a euphemism for sex when preceded by 'A bit of . . .'. Since this introduced a story about a girl who ran away with her teacher, no doubt the text producers are hoping the reader will make the connection. 'Snogs Ahoy!' is using an idiomatic phrase 'ship ahoy' and adapting it in a way which the reader will recognise.

Contractions occur when words are shortened:

the boy *spesh!* (*Bliss*)

Contractions, 'spesh' instead of 'special', are a feature of in-group language. This particular contraction is almost certainly recognisable by readers who fit the target age range of the magazine. Shortening words in this way suggests a familiarity with the reader.

Nominalisation is a process whereby a verb or verb group is turned into a noun. This is often found in reports of incidents where it might be advantageous to omit the agent, e.g. 'Police *shoot* demonstrators', may become 'Demonstrators die in *shooting*'. The following appeared in a magazine:

Gorgeous looks for your bathroom *(Bella)*

'Gorgeous looks' is an example of nominalisation. A process such as 'your bathroom looks gorgeous' is a temporary state or condition which has been changed to something more permanent, something to be worked upon. Again, there is no agent involved which makes it appear that 'your bathroom' will be transformed as if by magic.

Activity

Now see if you can spot which of these features occur in the following examples:

23

Bad boys

A man for all reasons

When the going gets tough the tough get even

'I'm dotty about Dale Winton'

Read my hips

Extension

Imagine you are the cover editor of a magazine. How would you present the following topics to your readers?

◎   A cookery feature on preparing vegetarian food for a special occasion.
◎   A fashion feature on 1950s-inspired clothes.

Commentary

The cookery feature on preparing vegetarian food appeared as THE GREEN PARTY and the fashion feature on fifties-inspired clothes as NEW SWEATER GIRL. Did your own headers resemble them in any way?

Summary

The vital role of the front cover can be summed up by the words of *Tatler's* editor: 'So there you have it. Worry about the front cover and the rest of the magazine will take care of itself - this month, at least.' The front cover acts as an advertisement for the magazine since it is the first text that the reader sees. We have looked at a wide range of linguistic techniques employed to grab our attention including rhyme, alliteration, assonance, superlatives, puns, intertextuality, idioms, contractions and nominalisation. We have also explored structural patterning with illustrations from a range of current front covers. Visual images and the different communities which readers are invited to join have also been covered.

Leafing through
The composition of the text

Aim of this unit

In this unit the aim is to look at how material is organised throughout the magazine and how individual pages are composed within it. This will include an examination of how the written text and visual images interact to convey information.

Front of house: the contents page

Because we read magazines in a non-linear fashion, the contents page is helpful for orientating the reader through the magazine. It leads the reader to the topics which are of interest to them, allowing them to skip others which they find less so. They can always come back to these if they wish.

The contents page has a set agenda which remains constant although the features themselves change from issue to issue. It is also useful for illustrating the range of genres which are included in magazines.

Activity

Have a look at the contents page of a magazine of your own choosing. Are you able to categorise the various features in any meaningful way?

Text : The importance of being a posh footballer

THE IMPORTANCE OF BEING A POSH FOOTBALLER

TATLER, June 1999   Photographed by Alexander Reilly

FOOTBALL IS SUPPOSED TO BE OUR NATIONAL GAME AND YET THE MEN WHO PLAY IT ARE ALMOST ALL WORKING CLASS. WHERE ARE THE PUKKA PLAYERS?

By OLIVIA STEWART-LIBERTY

The reason there aren't any posh footballers is that most posh schools don't play football. Calls to the top public schools revealed that Westminster and Eton, whose first sports are soccer, are in the minority. Gordonstoun describes football as its 'weakness', Bryanston admits to having

ETON
Tom Hudson

'no fixtures' and Rugby confirms that it's not called that for nothing. Posh boys are raised on the playing-field staples of hockey and rugby in winter, cricket and tennis in summer.

How can this be? Football is our national sport, and footballers are our national heroes. They pack out pubs when they appear on TV, and a glimpse inside their houses sells magazines. They're household names. They date our pop stars and TV personalities. They're the ones chosen to sell crisps, shampoo and pizza. In short, with their strong legs and seven-figure salaries, footballers are our new aristocracy.

Still, it is a rare Home Counties parent who is willing to back a

son's burning ambition to play professional football. First, there's no getting around the middle-class belief that sport is 'not a proper profession'. Most parents would greet their son's ambition with about as much enthusiasm as if he'd said he wanted to be a rock star. Football and footballers are not, in general, associated with wholesome, middle-class things. Take, for example, the widely documented, lager-fuelled antics of the pre-Priory Gazza. Or the black-eye pictures of Ulrika Jonsson and Sheryl Gascoigne taken after arguments with their respective footballer partners.

So, despite the fact that the middle classes contain some of football's most ardent and loyal supporters, it seems that there is no place for that class on the pitch. 'Football is a hard game,' acknowledges the Football Association, the game's governing body in this country. Too

FRENCH POLISH...
Ginola gives tactical tuition

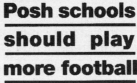

Posh schools should play more football

hard, it seems, for boys in the private-school sector. And yet, football was once the province of the public school. In the 1860s, Charterhouse and Westminster drafted the first set of rules for the FA Cup, and, in the 1870s and 1880s, Old Etonians, Old Carthusians and Oxford University actually won the trophy.

So, if what Tony Blair has said

is true, and England has become a 'middle-class' country, it seems strange that so few of the middle classes play soccer. It's probably time for posh schools to stop turning their noses up at the national sport, and time for football itself to stop turning its nose up at the middle classes. And then perhaps, with half the population no longer confined to the bench, one will be able to say, with conviction, that football is truly the 'people's game'.

'If my son wanted to play football, I'd encourage him like mad. It's a short, sharp career, but why not?'
THE DUKE OF WESTMINSTER
TAT STAT

152

26

EXCLUSIVE Ginola says 'Ooh la la' as football goes la-di-da

SEE NEXT PAGE

David Ginola wears Hawk overhead cagoule with reflective logo and taping, £75, colour block cargo pants, £45, both by Admiral. For details, see Stockists

GIN FIZZ... Eton's finest takes on the best Tottenham has to offer

CHARTERHOUSE
Matt Bailey

RADLEY
Tim Francis

MILLFIELD
Paul Heywood

FOREST
Nick Tester

WESTMINSTER
Elias Frangos

153

27

Commentary

Caldas-Coulthard (1996) found that the women's magazine *Marie Claire* had a fixed structure which was made up of eight major features:

1   Reportage – an article inspired by women's daily lives in other cultures
2   Profile – a celebrity interview
3   Emotional – a writer is commissioned to interview people about an emotional situation
4   Society – a slice of the social life
5   First person – a raw first-hand account of something that has happened to someone
6   Designer profile – a fashion story
7   Life stories – a mini-biography of a famous dead person
8   Review section – films, books, music, etc.

Did your content's page resemble this agenda in any way?

The composition of pages

Magazine articles vary in length and often several items are included on one page. Frequently there is a mixture of genres on the same page. The columns of text are often ragged in appearance, unlike the regularity of newspaper columns, with written text wrapped around visual images so that images and text work together. It is important to consider the visual images since the attractive pictures play such a large part in the magazine's appeal.

Activity

To illustrate the unique way in which magazine pages are composed it is interesting to compare them with the newspaper format which also belongs to the 'information giving' genre. Look at text: 'The importance of being a posh footballer', a feature which appeared in *Tatler*, a middle-class magazine. This feature is a parody of the *Sun's* sports pages. What differentiates this from a page layout of a magazine?

Left and right

The 'given' and the 'new'

The positioning of information on the page can itself convey meaning. Kress and VanLeeuwen (1996) examined double-page spreads in Australian women's magazines. They found that the right pages were 'dominated by large and salient photographs from which the gaze of one or more women engages the gaze of the viewer' (p. 186). These pictures often showed women in unusual or contradictory roles with which the reader is invited to identify. For example, the role might be a working woman who is shown coping with a 'tough', 'masculine' job. The left-hand pages, they found, usually comprised written text. From their analyses, Kress and VanLeeuwen concluded that there is a complementarity or continuous movement from left to right and that the right page was the site for 'key' or new information. What followed from this was that the left was the side of the 'already given': information which the reader already knows because they are a member of the culture (or rather the culture of the magazine). Although there was no such discernible pattern in the British magazines analysed for this book, Kress and VanLeeuwen's framework can usefully be applied, since it is clear that each page layout has been carefully designed. Kress and VanLeeuwen propose three principles of composition (1996: 183):

- Information value – the placement of elements, e.g. left and right, top and bottom, centre and margin, can endow them with specific informational value.
- Salience – The elements placed to attract the reader's attention to different degrees, e.g. foreground or background, relative size, contrasts in colour, sharpness, etc.
- Framing – The presence or absence of framing devices (dividing or framing lines), which connect or disconnect elements, signifying that they belong or do not belong together.

Activity

Look at text: 'The crazy, *crazy* world of international beauty queens' from *Cosmopolitan* and use the framework proposed to analyse the visual composition of the text.

The crazy, *crazy* world of international beauty queens

All over the globe, women are queuing to be crowned queen of, well, just about anything . . .

BY SASHA SLATER

This month, Miss UK will be crowned in Blackpool, scooping £7500 in prize money, plus guaranteed earnings of £20,000. She will have beaten over 10,000 others – and the number of contestants is on the up, says organiser Angie Beasley.

Beauty contests may be less fashionable, but they're more popular than ever. "It isn't only professional models who enter them," says Beasley. "We have doctors, lawyers and teachers too. The contest isn't just about what you look like."

Karen Fontaine, editor of *Pageanteer* magazine, estimates there are over 30,000 pageants in the US alone. "The number is growing every day as companies and tourist boards realise the publicity an attractive woman brings and more and more women realise how fun – and lucrative – competing is." Which means that, tall or short, fat or thin, ravishing beauty or just plain funny-looking, there's a contest out there for everyone.

Miss Batleys Cash And Carry
WHERE Yorkshire, UK.
WHEN Every 12 months, Batleys search for the female employee of the year.
WHO 15 contestants, one nominated by each warehouse.
JUDGED ON A questionnaire on their work and aspirations and photos.
PRIZE A TV and video.
REIGNING QUEEN Donna Stephenson, 31 (above).

Miss Peanut
WHERE Dotham, US.
WHO Entrants aged 17-21 from the peanut-producing counties in Florida and Georgia.
JUDGED ON An evening gown parade, an interview, school grades, writing skills and interests.
PRIZE Local shops offer clothes vouchers.
REIGNING QUEEN Brandy Holland, 21 (above). >

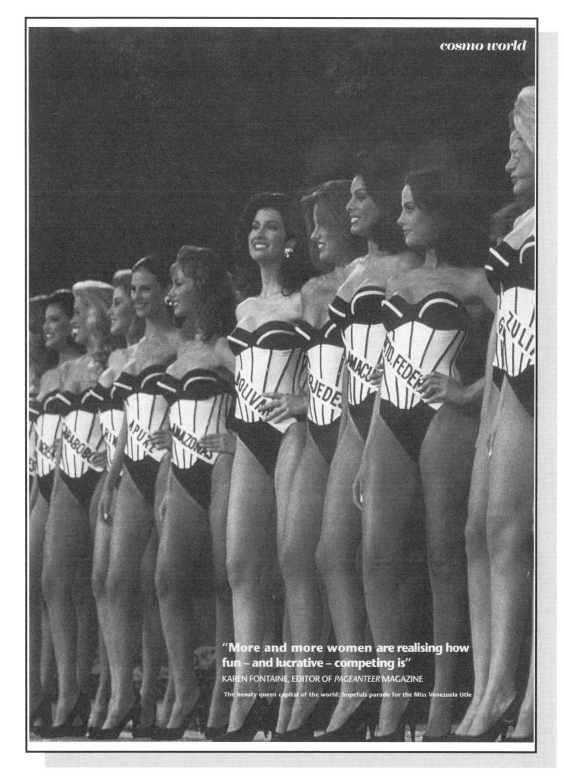

cosmo world

"More and more women are realising how fun – and lucrative – competing is"
KAREN FONTAINE, EDITOR OF *PAGEANTEER* MAGAZINE

The beauty queen capital of the world: hopefuls parade for the Miss Venezuela title

Commentary

The feature begins on a double page and continues over three pages. The right-hand side of the double page is dominated by a large picture of a beauty pageant. The image appears incompatible with the target audience of the magazine, which appeals to independent, career-orientated women, since the contestants are paraded like cattle, in identical swimsuits and appear to be the epitome of sex objects.

- ◎ Information value – placing the photograph of the beauty pageant to the right appears designed to provoke the audience – they are led to the written text in an attempt to identify the purpose for including such obviously sexist material in a magazine which targets independent, career-orientated women.
- ◎ Salience – the images are in focus at the beginning of the line-up which starts at the right-hand margin. As this tapers, the relative size of the contestants diminishes and their faces blur, again leading the reader towards the written text. The header, 'The crazy, *crazy* world of international beauty queens', shows some attempt at colour co-ordination has been made since the letters match the flesh tones of the beauty contestants.
- ◎ Framing – the large visual image appears to be framed by the header which begins in the top left-hand corner, 'The crazy, *crazy* world of international beauty queens', and a satellite text which appears opposite in the bottom right-hand corner, '"More and more women are realising how fun – and lucrative – competing is".' The messages appear to be contradictory since, on the one hand, the text producer is acknowledging that the world of beauty contests is 'crazy', but this is counterpoised with the quotation which points out the financial gains to be had from entering beauty contests. The effect of these contrasting views is to cancel each other out, leaving the reader to make up her own mind.

Top and bottom

The 'ideal' and the 'real'

With reference to advertisements, Kress and VanLeeuwen found that the upper section visualised 'the promise of the product' (the ideal), and the lower section provided factual information about the product (the real). They found there to be less connection between the two parts of the

"Grinning like a loon won't get you off doing the dishes, love."

The Vintage Magazine Co.

"We're an item"

Does the sight of a publicly-kissing couple make you want to throw a bucket of water over them? Michael Bracewell finds flaws in smug twosomes

Have you ever noticed how the couples in TV adverts tend to behave in precisely the opposite way to couples in real life? How many half-way rational couples do you know who laugh uproariously every time someone hands them a plate of pasta, or exchange mischievous glances with an unseen third party whenever they take the cap off a bottle of bathroom cleaner? As most men know, couples in real life tend to eat pasta in moody silence because one of them has left it in the pan for too long and it's gone all chewy. In short, trying to do all of the things which the happy, well-adjusted couples with self-cleaning teeth do in adverts can be a constant struggle.

So before you put on matching cardigans and assume the spooky smiles of people who are in deep shock, consider the reality which lies behind those 'ideal couple' moments:

Doing pointless things

Somehow, once you're in a couple you are allowed to do entirely pointless things which a single person would conceal as evidence of their sad and lonely lives. Say to a beaming couple, "What did you do on Sunday?" and they'll reply with tremendous enthusiasm that they "went for a walk". "Where to?" you enquire, hoping that this will extract an interesting fact. "Oh, nowhere special," responds the loving couple.

In fact, the more pointless a couple's activity, the more it is evidence that they are deeply in love. There are even couples who just sit in a room and stare at one another. They might try to pass this off in public as proof of their infatuation with one another, but it would only take the addition of one of them locking the door and the police would probably get involved. If you are in a couple,

and are just getting used to loving the way she simmers her sprouts, try to spare a thought for the unattached observers of your bliss. Tone down your care-free existence by adding the words "to the bottle bank" after "we just went for a walk". It may spare someone's feelings.

Remembering birthdays

A man will know that he's really one half of a couple when his girlfriend starts handing him birthday cards inscribed to people he's never heard of and demanding that he sign his name next to hers. The co-signed card is seen to imply that a couple has crossed the threshold of maturity.

One of life's little mysteries must be why women tend to think that sending jointly-signed birthday cards is the relationship equivalent of passing your driving test or ▷

composition in texts which make use of the top and bottom of the page than in texts which use the left and right but there is, they say, a contrast, some kind of opposition between the two parts. The text "'We're an item'" from *Men's Health* shows in the top section a picture of a 'happy, well-adjusted couple with self cleaning teeth' (whatever that might mean). The written text certainly acts in opposition since it lampoons couples who are in love, largely due to their smugness. The visual image is from a very dated advertisement, perhaps reminding the reader of old-fashioned standards. The written text, in contrast, produces a sense that we are living in more enlightened times. In acknowledging the artificial nature of advertisements, that couples in real life do not behave like the couples in advertisements, the text producer is addressing an enlightened reader. However, he also recognises that advertisers are still using the same tricks in modern adverts:

> How many half-way rational couples do you know who laugh uproariously every time someone hands them a plate of pasta, or exchange mischievous glances with an unseen third party whenever they take the cap off a bottle of bathroom cleaner?

These are references to current advertisements which seem to tell us that nothing much has changed, merely we are more aware of advertisers' ploys.

Centre and margin

According to Kress and VanLeeuwen, the centre zone of the page has a symbolic value, often unifying what surrounds the image. This may be seen in the text: 'It's a man's world' from *Men's Health*. The page has seven boxes of equal size, each box containing an image of a men's grooming product. A large section of the centre zone is taken up with the header and subtext. This is placed on the left-hand side of the page. Conventionally, cosmetics are not associated with men so it may seem odd, at first sight, to find a promotional feature which aims to advertise cosmetics in a men's magazine. Using the framework outlined, the centre zone, which has the large letters 'it's a man's world', would appear designed to unify the apparent contradiction of the surrounding images: the various beauty products. The header is a well-known saying, 'It's a man's world', which emphasises a view that men dominate society, the given; and the new idea that cosmetics can be part of 'a man's world' because 'real men', whatever that might mean, are now using cosmetics.

Text : It's a man's world

MEN'S HEALTH PROMOTION

Eau de Toilette for Men.
Part of the new Harrods for Men collection.

Origins Fire Fighter. Soothes post-shave burning.

Origins Blade Runner.
Energizing Shave Cream for a friction-free shave.

it's a man's world

It's official, real men use cosmetics. And, as these innovative products from the Men's Grooming Room at Harrods prove, there are lots of great gifts out there that not only smell good and perform well, but look super cool in your bathroom cabinet

Molton Brown Ultra-Light Hydrator. Great for cooling sensitive post-shave skin. Oil free.

Philosophy Razor Sharp. A light shaving gel which combines soothing aloe vera and silicone for a smoother shave.

Philosophy The Afterglow. Oil free, smoothing gel. Revitalises skin by sweeping away dead cells.

Hermès Rocabar. A woody, balmy fragrance in a masculine, geometrical bottle, wrapped in a mini blanket.

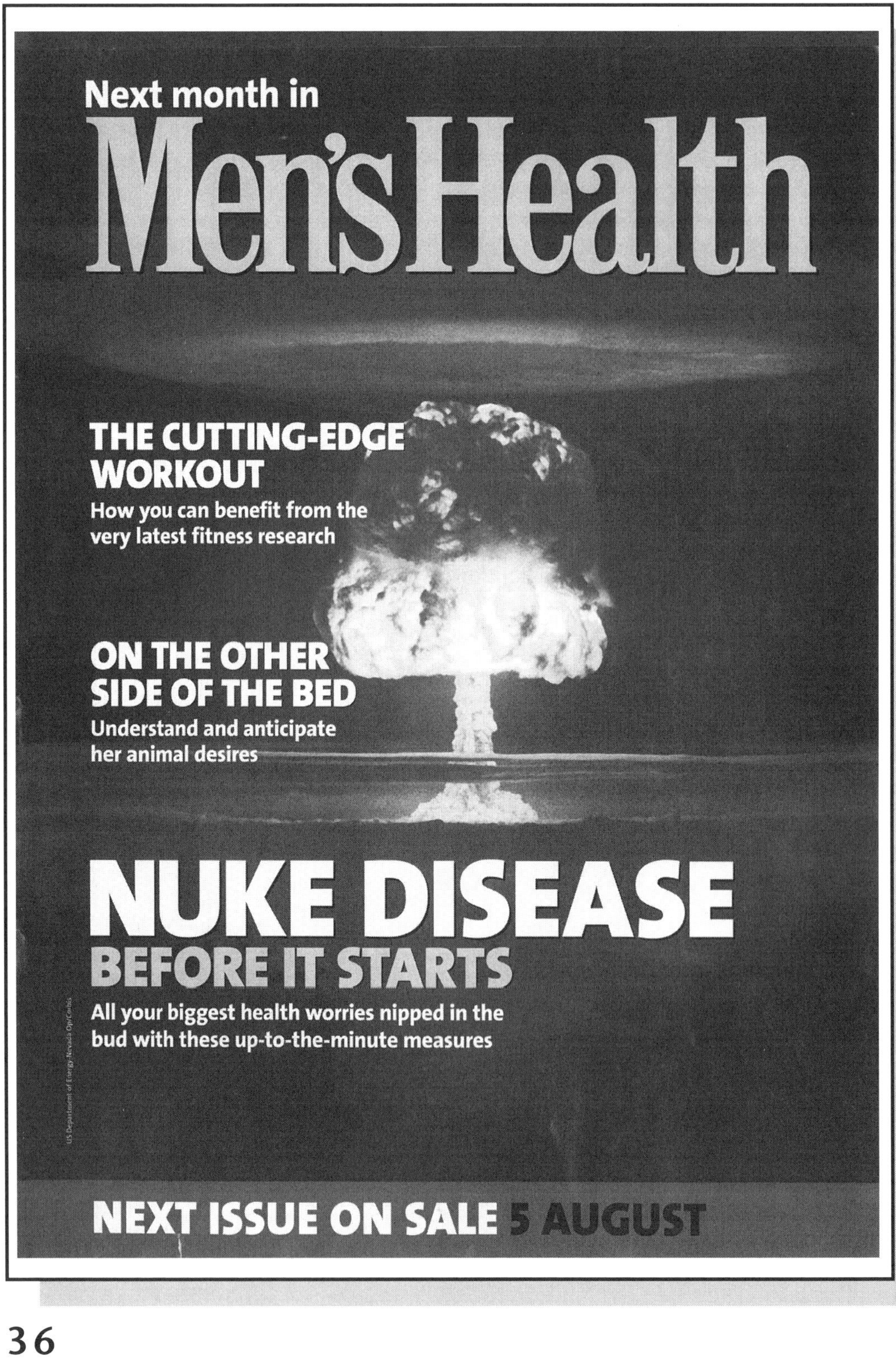
Next month in
Men's Health
THE CUTTING-EDGE
WORKOUT
How you can benefit from the
very latest fitness research
ON THE OTHER
SIDE OF THE BED
Understand and anticipate
her animal desires
NUKE DISEASE
BEFORE IT STARTS
All your biggest health worries nipped in the
bud with these up-to-the-minute measures
NEXT ISSUE ON SALE 5 AUGUST

Note the careful choice of vocabulary: 'grooming' rather than 'beauty'; the text producer can only go so far.

Coincidentally, the opposite page also makes use of the centre. This is an advertisement for the forthcoming issue of the magazine.

Activity

Look at text: 'Next month in *Men's Health*'. Is there a symbolic/informational value in the page layout?

Commentary

This particular front cover is a detour from the usual image of a muscular male model. The text producer is taking quite a risk in breaking with the structural pattern familiar to readers. The central image shows the mushroom cloud of a nuclear fallout. The colours of the background and image are contrasted in the surrounding written text. The title of the magazine is in the same colour as the centre of the fallout. The largest heading which is placed just below the image states: 'Nuke Disease Before it Starts'. It seems that the text producer has taken the idea of nuclear warfare and related the metaphor with a view to 'nipping in the bud' readers' health worries. The masculine connotations associated with war reaffirm masculinity which might otherwise be eroded by mentioning male anxiety.

Summary

This unit has attempted to show how the overall organisation of the material inside magazines, by keeping to a fixed structure, sets up the reader's expectations of what is to come in future editions. It has also demonstrated by examining the composition of pages that the written text and visual images often, as in the examples above, work together to produce meaning.

Extension

As more and more magazines are producing their own web sites, an interesting project might be to look at how web pages are composed,

37

whether they differ from the hard copy and if so in what ways. One of the web sites visited for the purpose of this book was *FHM*. Obvious differences were that instead of turning over pages icons had to be clicked. The use of animation is a feature which technology has made possible and something which the composers of web pages have taken on board.

Whether you think this is an advance will depend on how you view the change from still images used to show, for example, various postures for having sex in 'Position of the fortnight', to moving ones.

The following list of website addresses might whet your appetite. You might also like to look at the *Intertext* page on the Routledge website for updates on this series.

FHM	http://www.fhm.com
GQ	http://www.gq-magazine.co.uk
Men's Health	http://www.men's health.co.uk
Tatler	http://www.tatler.co.uk

In-house
Magazine contents

Aim of this unit

The aim of this unit is to examine the contents of magazines and to consider also what is excluded and who decides on this in terms of the editorial processes.

What is the purpose of magazines? The answer to this depends on from whose viewpoint the question is posed. On the reader's part, primarily they are to entertain us, hence the abundance of linguistic tools mentioned in Units two and three. Magazines are also informative, telling us about the latest products on offer. They can be instructional, e.g. the 'how to' genre which was mentioned in the introduction. On the text producer's part they are a vehicle for promoting various commodities through advertisements because this is where the real revenue lies. Money from the actual sales of magazines is quite negligible.

Our examination of the contents page in unit three demonstrated that magazines can be characterised by their heterogeneity. It also showed, by the large number of advertisements, that the purpose of magazines is to sell the commodities advertised; often by persuading us in the various features that we are in need of them. Even those features which do not on the surface appear to be selling anything, e.g. the interest in the personal lives of celebrities, interviews, etc., keep us informed about the latest films, concert tours, CDs and so on which are available for purchase.

The next section will examine some of the regular features which appear in magazines.

39

Horoscopes

Horoscopes are predictions of people's future based on the zodiac (an imaginary belt which contains the twelve zodiacal constellations) for the time of their birth. In magazines they are usually accompanied by symbols and dates. The signs of the zodiac have cultural connotations, for example scales are often used to represent the sign Libra, fish are used to represent Pisces, etc.

Activity

Look at the star signs accompanying the *Bella* horoscopes and compare them with those of *Bliss*. What connotations are implied?

Your stars

For the week
22 — 29 August 1998
By Nick Campion

Virgo
24 Aug — 23 Sept
Easy does it! Your ideas are on line, your desires on track and your plans look good. But maybe you should keep certain things secret to avoid unfair criticism.

Scorpio
24 Oct — 22 Nov
Although you'll keep partners up to date on many of your plans, you'll still hold something back. Make sure uncomfortable facts don't leak out bit by bit.

Capricorn
23 Dec — 20 Jan
Developments will focus on financial possibilities. You're either about to discover business potential, with remarkable results, or you're going on a shopping spree!

Libra
24 Sept — 23 Oct
We will all benefit from your love of beauty, for behind your sensitivity, you're struggling to make your environment a nicer, happier and more peaceful place.

Sagittarius
23 Nov — 22 Dec
Look far afield for inspiration — it's a time for adventure, even global travel. However, if you decide to stay at home, find every way you can to mix with new people.

Aquarius
21 Jan — 19 Feb
Although you may be reliving former memories, you can now break free from emotional ties which are more burden than joy. Wednesday is a great day for true love.

The Sun is now in Virgo, a much misunderstood sign. Sure, Virgos can be fussy people, but they're not just being needlessly picky. They're perfectionists and aren't ready to settle for anything less then the best. But don't worry — they're as hard on themselves as they are on you!

Pisces
20 Feb — 20 Mar
The Sun meets Saturn in one of its sober alignments, so you'll get on best if you're sensible. Midweek brings near perfect conditions for financial deals.

Taurus
21 April — 21 May
You'll be doing whatever you can to acquire respect from friends and neighbours. Once you've organised events, you will have greater satisfaction.

Cancer
22 June — 23 July
You're strong on commonsense when totting up figures. You'll make a shrewd deal and anyone trying to overcharge could end up owing you money!

Aries
21 Mar — 20 April
This is one of the most productive phases of the year. You're now contemplating promotion at work, but it's equally important that you advance private passions.

Gemini
22 May — 21 June
If I could list your better qualities at the moment, they'd include your lively and friendly attitude — and your extraordinary willingness to try whatever life offers you.

Leo
24 July — 23 Aug
There has rarely been a time when your horoscope was so full of bounce. Energetic and passionate, others will follow your lead. Listen to your instincts.

Text: *Bliss!* horoscopes

Arien luck alert

Lucky Day: Tuesday

Lucky Gemstone: Diamond

Lucky Charm: A diamond brooch

Compatible Celebs: Will Mellor (Aries) AJ Backstreet (Leo) Isaac Hanson (Sagittarius)

Taurus
(21 April – 21 May)

You: Why are you torturing yourself so, Taurus? What has happened has happened and it's high time you let it go. Everyone else has forgotten about it, so why don't you?

Love: You're in the position to play matchmaker this month, but don't try to fix your mate up with the guy you fancy yourself. If you do you may well live to regret it later.

Cosmic diary dates:
Laugh it off: 5th.
Parent problems: 13th.
Go for it: 27th

Cancer
(22 June – 23 July)

You: Life may be a little more complicated than usual this month. Whatever happens, it's wise to remember that honesty is the best policy – even if it means dumping someone in it.

Love: This month a close friend of yours may try

to pair you off with a bloke she knows. Try not to get too excited though – the stars suggest that he isn't a heavenly match for you.

Cosmic diary dates:
Turn him down: 3rd.
Keep a straight face: 12th
School hassle: 19th.

Leo
(24 July – 23 August)

You: It really isn't your fault your mate is being narky with everyone right now. Give her a wide berth for a couple of days – she'll soon calm down and apologise. She may need a friend to talk to, so be patient and be there for her.

Love: Sick of being single? Worried that you'll die a grumpy old spinster? Worry not, because the

stars this month suggest that soon after the 13th someone is likely to make your heart flutter.

Cosmic diary dates:
No time like the present: 2nd.
Smoocharama: 15th.
Just do it: 29th.

Libra
(24 September – 23 October)

You: Everything seems to be going your way and, with the help of the cosmos behind you, nothing is going to stop you from reaching your goal.

Love: You're so caught up with life that love may have to take a back seat. However, if you already

have a lad don't push for any type of commitment just yet, because the stars suggest he'll run a mile if you do.

Cosmic diary dates:
It's up to you: 4th.
Listen to your mates: 17th.
Forget it: 26th.

Scorpio
(24 October – 22 November)

You: You have every right to be angry, but spreading rumours about someone else isn't the way to get them back. They'll get their comeuppance soon, so don't stoop to their level.

Love: Don't bottle your emotions up, Scorpio. If he's hurt your feelings let him know – he's not a mind reader, you know. Besides, if you let him he'll do it again and again.

Cosmic diary dates:
Consider all options: 1st.
A brief encounter: 7th.
Be nice, help others: 25th.

Capricorn

(22 December – 20 January)

You: Fun-loving planets put you in the mood to party, but be very careful who you hang out with after the 13th because troublesome planetary aspects could see you getting into a bit of bother.

Love: You may want to broaden your boy horizons  this month as the stars suggest you'll fancy older lads. They may seem cool but get involved with one this month and it could be more trouble than it's worth.

Cosmic diary dates:
Ring the changes: 3rd.
Beware, beauty is only skin deep: 13th.
Be very cautious: 30th.

Aquarius

(21 January – 19 February)

You: It takes time to do things properly and being impatient only means that you'll have to do things more than once. Take a deep breath and let destiny take you by the hand. You're almost there.

Love: You're impatient when it comes to love and  your desperation for a boyfriend could see you heading down heartbreak avenue. Your perfect boy is just around the corner, so hang on in there.

Cosmic diary dates:
Time to party: 9th.
No way: 14th.
Sock it to 'em: 29th.

Gemini

(22 May – 21 June)

You: You're in the mood to strike out on your own because you're sick of being treated like a kid – hmmph! Give it a couple more months and your folks will start seeing things your way.

Love: You're in the mood to shove your tongue down the throat of the first guy you meet this  month. But obviously you need to restrain this urge otherwise you could get yourself a reputation!

Cosmic diary dates:
Be straight: 10th.
Time to trust your instincts: 22nd.
Snog him: 30th.

Sagittarius

(23 November – 21 December)

You: You're faced with a couple of difficult decisions this month and there's no getting away from making them. It might seem quite scary now but this time next month you'll be wondering what all the fuss was about.

Love: Saucy planets are making you hot under the  collar. However, if you already have a lad you'll need to avoid the temptation to get off with someone else!

Cosmic diary dates:
Plan for the future: 3rd.
Reconsider: 10th.
Seek and you shall find: 27th.

Virgo

(24 August – 23 September)

You: Is this what you really want? Thought not. Take a step back and reorganise your priorities. You may have to upset a few people but your happiness is far more important right now.

Love: You've been sitting by the phone waiting for  him to ring for far too long. Rather than moping about, why not ring him yourself? The stars suggest that he'll be really pleased to hear from you. You just need to be brave and go for it.

Cosmic diary dates:
The time is near: 4th.
Tread carefully: 12th.
Have a laugh: 17th.

Pisces

(20 February – 20 March)

You: It's at times like these that you need your friends the most. Things may look bleak but life isn't as bad as it seems. Talking your worries through might help you see things differently.

Love: Be very careful because guys you meet this month may not be what they seem. Even though they may promise you the earth, the chance of them delivering is very slim indeed.

Cosmic diary dates:
Watch it: 6th.
Take it: 15th.
Buy it: 26th.

Commentary

Did you notice that the sign for Libra in *Bliss* shows a pair of legs on bathroom scales whereas in Bella they are the more traditional style, often used to symbolise the scales of justice? This also fits in with another name for Libra which is 'Balance'. The signs in *Bliss* are quite amusing, which is in keeping with its youthful and fun image, but on a more serious note the images of slim young women which proliferate on the front cover and within the magazine perhaps encourage weight consciousness. You might consider why *Cosmopolitan* chooses not to use symbols for illustration (see Text: *Cosmopolitan* on pp. 46–7). Perhaps they are considered to be unsophisticated for that particular magazine. It is also interesting to question why, at the time of writing, horoscopes are absent from men's magazines. Unit seven covers a range of genres and topics which were previously thought to be 'off limits' to men, so this too could change.

Activity

To help you recognise just how formulaic the horoscope genre is you could try writing your own. Here's a first line to get you started:

The Sun meets Saturn in one of its sober alignments, so you'll get on best if you're sensible. . . .

What expectations did you have of horoscopes? What choices of language did you make? Were they appropriate for the genre? How did your text compare with the following? Text: A is from a student and Text: B is from *Bella* magazine:

Text: A

The Sun meets Saturn in one of its sober alignments, so you'll get on best if you're sensible. If you are planning to go on holiday make sure you pack a cossie and not that indecent bikini. You may already have a partner who you share your life with, but for single Arians this could be the ideal time to find someone to share your universe with. You are about to make big strides in your career so you can feel that all the hard work has been worth it.

Text: B

Libra
24 Sept — 23 Oct
We will all benefit from your love of beauty, for behind your sensitivity, you're struggling to make your environment a nicer, happier and more peaceful place.

Horoscopes are very personal yet they are addressed to many people. You will see that the text producers of horoscopes attempt two things: first, to present people with a positive self-image to aspire to – 'We will all benefit from your love of beauty, for behind your sensitivity…' – and, second, to get them to change some negative aspects about themselves – 'you'll get on best if you're sensible'. You can see this is achieved largely through flattery. Considering that the text producer does not know the reader personally, you might be surprised at the verb patterns used. From the examples given, the text producers appear quite assured in their opinion which is reflected by the modal auxiliary 'will' – 'We will all benefit…' – and the primary auxiliary verb 'are' in 'you're struggling'. You will also notice lexis which is quite specific to astrology such as the names of planets and their movements: 'The Sun meets Saturn in one of its sober alignments, so you'll get on best if you're sensible.' Here the planets are **personified** (endowed with human characteristics): we imagine them to be old acquaintances meeting sedately and rationally ('sober') rather than their implied customary drunken state.

Text : *Cosmopolitan* horoscopes

september

Love, life and career – the most important aspects of your star sign for the month ahead. BY MAGGIE HYDE

libra 23 SEPTEMBER – 22 OCTOBER

CAREER Everything you do just creates more work. And because there's so much to do, you can't get organised. Prioritise, and don't work a 24-hour day or your health will suffer.

MONEY Whether you need a cleaner or a homeopath, don't be afraid to spend on people who can make your life easier.

LOVE You are at your most critical while Venus travels through perfectionist Virgo, but don't demand too much from a man. Tone down your idealism and work with the clay you have.

SILENCES Waging a war of silence with another female, possibly a sister, makes you anxious. Talk to her and clear the air.

Month ahead: 0891 336571*

scorpio

23 OCTOBER – 21 NOVEMBER

CAREER While Mars is in proud Leo, take a confident approach. If your boss is unreasonable, avoid an open challenge as the truth of a situation will become obvious.

MONEY Your ambivalence about a big buy is making your partner nervous. Make a decision – and stick to it.

LOVE Be patient with a man if a niggle about something petty turns into a row. There are deeper issues to work through, and blame doesn't help anyone.

INDULGE Stop calorie-counting for once and let a friend tempt you into a little self-indulgence. It will relieve stress.

Month ahead: 0891 336572*

sagittarius

22 NOVEMBER – 21 DECEMBER

CAREER Behind-the-scenes deals could leave you out of the picture; don't overreact on the basis of limited information.

MONEY Spending on a car could be blown out of proportion early in the month. Avoid sentiment and tot up the final costs.

LOVE A conflict involving a lover or a

virgo 23 AUGUST – 22 SEPTEMBER

CAREER More hard work is not enough. Cultivate personal contacts so the right people start to know your face – then they'll take an interest in what you have to offer.

MONEY Face the truth (and your bank statement) on the 25th. The situation may be worse than it ought to be, but it's a lot better than it could be.

LOVE The lunar eclipse on the 6th threatens misunderstandings between you and a man. This is a passing phase, so don't be melodramatic.

KNOW-HOW Acquiring new skills means making a small commitment now for big returns later.

Month ahead: 0891 336570*

Celebrity birthday: Cameron Diaz, 30 August 1972
Other Virgo icons: Claudia Schiffer, Stella McCartney, Ricki Lake, Raquel Welch

Candid Cameron: keeping up the contacts in September

family member makes you want to run away. Work out where your loyalty lies.

NO JOKE A friend teasing you about something you've been putting off shouldn't annoy you – it should spur you into action.

Month ahead: 0891 336573*

capricorn

22 DECEMBER – 19 JANUARY

CAREER Past efforts pay off and you have several new options. Don't be influenced by status – doing what you love is important.

MONEY You're shocked at your spending

COSMO TAROT PHONELINE

The *Cosmopolitan* Tarot Phoneline can be used for a general reading, but it's best to focus on a specific issue. Your call will click you into a three-card reading. Maggie Hyde will explain the meaning of each card and suggest your way forward. Have a pen and paper to hand, so you can make a note of your cards and think about them afterwards.

Call the Cosmopolitan Tarot Phoneline on 0891 666075*

and angry with a partner for wasting resources. Take it in hand around the 4th.

LOVE You'll feel down because you and a man seem poles apart, but it's this month's eclipse distorting your perception. Overall, you have plenty in common.

MORAL DILEMMAS Despite the pressure others put on you, stick to your principles.

Month ahead: 0891 336574*

aquarius

20 JANUARY – 18 FEBRUARY

CAREER A new phase is starting, but learn to walk before you can run. Someone with expert knowledge helps around the 29th.

MONEY Organise debts, particularly on a credit card, before they become a burden.

LOVE Compromises with your partner mean creative goals are on hold. If your relationship is to work, he has to recognise your needs are as important as his.

SHOCK TACTIC Someone close to you upsets you. But they don't mean to hurt, they just want some attention.

Month ahead: 0891 336575*

pisces 19 FEBRUARY – 19 MARCH

CAREER Routines are not your forte, but >

***COSMOLINES:** *Calls cost 50p per minute. The numbers can be reached only by callers in the UK and the Channel Islands.*

PHOTOGRAPHS ALL ACTION: TONY STONE

46

horoscopes

< having a system would make you feel much more in control. Revamp your approach to work with help from a smart man.

MONEY Your partner gets a bonus or windfall around the 9th and wants you to share it. Why refuse?

LOVE A change in image has a dramatic effect on your attractiveness. But if you were born in the first week of March, the Moon's eclipse could bring trouble from a partner's ex.

OLD FRIENDS A friend you haven't seen for years turns up again and it's as if he has never been away.

Month ahead: 0891 336576*

aries 20 MARCH – 19 APRIL

CAREER Rushing through jobs to get them out of the way is a waste of time if you mess things up and have to start again. Get it right first time round.

MONEY Self-disciplined Saturn gives you control over your cash. With planning, you can afford everything you want.

LOVE You are happy alone until around the 23rd, when a new relationship seems to spring out of nowhere. You *hate* obsessing about a man, but somehow you just can't help it.

RISKY Taking a risk to get something you have always wanted is thrilling, but it won't please a friend.

Month ahead: 0891 336565*

taurus 20 APRIL – 20 MAY

CAREER While Venus is in practical Virgo, respond to immediate pressures at work rather than fix on long-term goals. Stepping in to clear up a mess earns you extra Brownie points around the 9th.

MONEY You earned it, now spend it – especially on clothes or beauty treatments that enhance your style.

LOVE You're in a playful mood, but you could underestimate the effect you have on a man. Don't promise a three-course meal if you're only up for starters.

WAR ZONE Someone wants to have an argument, but if you get dragged in there's no knowing where it will end.

Month ahead: 0891 336566*

gemini 21 MAY – 20 JUNE

CAREER The Moon's eclipse puts a damper on things at work. Even your boss seems to have lost the plot. Be a typically cool and rational Gemini and you can

help others to get through all the turmoil.

MONEY Spending on your home is soaring, but borrowing to buy new furniture isn't the answer to your problem.

LOVE After the 24th, get out, have some fun and attract a fascinating new man, probably a Scorpio. But watch out for his emotional sting.

TALENT You've always been good at art, so develop your gifts.

Month ahead: 0891 336567*

cancer 21 JUNE – 22 JULY

CAREER Your paperwork is a nightmare, because you haven't got all the facts. But don't struggle on your own: get a superior involved and let them struggle, too.

MONEY A spending spree is coming to an end, but there's still one more must-have. If it really is essential, the sooner you buy it, the sooner you can make up for the financial damage.

LOVE A relationship you thought you were free of is back, and it's creating

confusion. You can't avoid being drawn in, but do remind yourself how addictive this man really is – and why.

WRONG PATH You're off-beam with your plans for a travel or educational venture and opportunities aren't what they seem.

Month ahead: 0891 336568*

leo 23 JULY – 22 AUGUST

CAREER 'Can do, will do' is your motto, but don't underestimate opposition from an unexpected quarter on the 4th.

MONEY Early in the month is a tricky time to arrange a loan or get a mortgage. Wait and you'll get a fairer deal.

LOVE An intimate relationship clicks into gear when you a suss out a man's desires. You may have to overcome years of male-ego conditioning before he'll give priority to his emotions.

NET LOSS A holiday acquaintance is now keeping things going by e-mail, but if he's boring, don't be afraid to erase him.

Month ahead: 0891 336569*

Great taste?

Some signs have a natural sense of style. How do you score in the taste stakes?

casual wear doesn't let you down. (6/10)

CAPRICORN Classic styles show you have taste, but spice things up with colour to show off your creative flare. (7/10)

AQUARIUS Tastelessly extreme one day, and breathtakingly stylish the next – you're in a class of your own. (5/10)

PISCES You don't have an eye for detail, but your amazing eye for colour is a bonus. Plan more, and go shopping with a Virgo friend. (5/10)

ARIES Garish colours, gimmicks and impulse buys create style clashes. Be adventurous, but keep it simple. (5/10)

VIRGO You show style and class in everything, from your clothes and your car to tiny objects in your home. (10/10)

LIBRA You have a superb ability to mix, match and co-ordinate, but don't be a fashion victim. (9/10)

SCORPIO Your tendency to overdress can come across as bad taste. Exploit your natural sex appeal, yes, but keep it simple. (5/10)

SAGITTARIUS You look great when you dress up, but make sure your

TAURUS You buy the best you can afford. Your colour sense is subtle and you go for clothes that look *and* feel good. (8/10)

GEMINI You're a sucker for trends and know how to wear them. Stick with the cheap and cheerful, as you chuck things out so quickly. But remember the importance of investment pieces. (6/10)

CANCER You love pastels and look good in them, but a few sober, masculine touches would go a long way. (5/10)

LEO You are elegant and flamboyant, but don't confuse extravagance with taste. Go easy on the big jewellery. (7/10)

***COSMOLINES:** Calls cost 50p per minute. The numbers can be reached only by callers in the UK and the Channel Islands.*

ARIES
21 March – 20 April

Planets in Sagittarius tickle your sense of humour and put any problems to the back of your mind. Your imagination is running wild, and if you can echo that by being adventurous in real life, you'll feel fulfilled. A steady relationship is a mixed blessing: you're passionate and uninhibited but may dislike routine. **Hot date:** 1 December

If he's Aries He's dreaming of strangers and far-away places. Cloak yourself in mystery to hold his interest! If you share his impulsive attitude to life you'll enjoy his experiments. No two days are the same! He's discovering new talents and chances to combine them with work could crop up at the end of November. **Hot date:** 24 November

TAURUS
21 April – 21 May

Being unsure of your direction is making you cling a bit too hard to anything or anyone that represents security. Think before making demands of friends – they don't exist just to help you with your problems. Financial good luck on 22 November points the way to success. Positive thinking gets easier after the 27th. **Hot date:** 25 November

If he's Taurus Though he may seem quiet and thoughtful he'll bare his soul if you give him half a chance. Don't let him get away with just talking, though. A few firm decisions are needed. Passionate sex is a great outlet for his frustrations, and he'll get more indulgent generally in December. **Hot date:** 4 December

GEMINI
22 May – 21 June

Five planets ganging up in the area of your chart influencing love and friendship this fortnight make you highly attuned to other people's thoughts and desires. You know who you want, you know who wants you, and you've got the confidence to be direct. Telling someone the truth on 23 November could hurt. **Hot date:** 27 November

If he's Gemini He's a real flirt, but with serious motives. There's nothing trivial about his feelings this fortnight. He's prepared to be honest, intimate and trusting and wants the same in return. He won't be nearly so casual as usual about lateness or being let down, though, so stay on your toes. **Hot date:** 27 November

CANCER
22 June – 23 July

The spotlight is on work that makes you feel good and useful, but doesn't necessarily make you richer! You'll get a bit more balance back towards the end of November when Venus and Mars move into Capricorn, hotting up your love life. You've given lots out, now it's time to take something back. **Hot date:** 24 November

If he's Cancer If he doesn't realise how often he's letting you down in order to do a favour for a complete stranger, put him in the picture! He's such a saint these days, though, that he might seem beyond criticism. He's been spreading himself quite thin and secretly longs for you to insist on having him to yourself. **Hot date:** 29 November

LEO
24 July – 23 August

The Sun crossing paths with Mercury and Pluto on 23 November brings chaos to your social life. Change is a little scary, but the phase you're entering is important. You're more mature, you're taking the initiative, and though you've outgrown some friends, new relationships are blossoming. **Hot date:** 26 November

If he's Leo He's loving and sensual, and he'll tell you exactly how he's feeling, even if it isn't quite what you want to hear. He's giving you a chance to accept or reject him: he wants to be with people who love him for what he is. That's not to say he won't change, but if he does, the impulse must come from within himself. **Hot date:** 23 November

VIRGO
24 August – 23 September

Planets in the home area of your chart make security and happiness a priority. You might feel that events will run along at their own pace, no matter what you do, but you underestimate your calming effect. You can have a lot of fun this week by inviting people to come to you instead of always going to them. **Hot date:** 4 December

If he's Virgo He wants to get to the root of what you think and how you feel, and you could find his questions disconcerting. It's not that he's always serious, he just won't let you get away with a quick answer. He feels that the more he knows, the more control he has. And he wants to be in control. **Hot date:** 30 November

LIBRA
24 September – 23 October

You're in demand. Your family is constantly asking you for help and advice. Your friends know you're a mine of information. Libran charm is a great man magnet, especially when you're using it as confidently as you are right now. And your talent as a great communicator gets you noticed at work, too. **Hot date:** 2 December

If he's Libra He's full of good intentions, but how is he going to fit in romantic moments with all his other commitments? He's a real hit with people this fortnight, smoothing out their troubles and making them laugh. Your best bet for a passionate smooch is on 22 November when sensual Venus and Mars cross paths. **Hot date:** 28 November

SCORPIO
24 October – 22 November

The disruptive conjunction of Pluto, Mercury and the Sun on 23 November affects areas of your life that you take for granted. You may look at your job or your home and suddenly realise that it has to change. Scorpios can make bold starts out of tough situations, so take a deep breath and do what has to be done. **Hot date:** 29 November

If he's Scorpio To say he's preoccupied is an understatement! He's having to weigh up what he wants and when he wants it, and he may feel that if he doesn't get it right this time he won't get another chance. He's in the mood for commitments, so if you've been longing to tell him how much you care, go for it! **Hot date:** 3 December

Activity

You might imagine that horoscopes are targeted at anyone who is born under a particular star sign, but by examining the language of the selection of horoscopes we can see that the text producers have a particular reader in mind. Consider these questions: Does the text address the reader directly by using the pronouns 'you/your' and 'I /we'? Does the text address the reader as female/male? What assumptions are made about the reader?

Commentary

Text: *Cosmopolitan* horoscope
The reference to working a 24-hour day is addressed to a professional, career-minded person. The reader is explicitly addressed as a woman in 'Waging a war of silence with *another* female . . .'
Text: *Bliss* horoscope (see p. 42)
A presupposition is made about the reader's sexuality, namely that she is heterosexual and in favour of monogamous relationships: 'If you already have *a lad* . . .' Young women are urged to modify their behaviour in order to prioritise the needs of males: 'don't push for any type of commitment just yet, because the stars suggest he'll run a mile if you do.' Also, in *Bliss*, friends figure quite prominently: 'Listen to your mates . . .'
Text: *More!* horoscope
The horoscopes in *More!* are oriented towards sex, e.g. 'great man magnet', 'passionate smooch', 'sensual Venus'. Indeed they are introduced as 'horny horoscopes' which fits in with the ethos of the magazine.

Reader's letters

The letters page provides a forum for the readers to interact with the magazine's text producers and other readers.

Activity

Look at the texts: readers' letters. These are just some examples for illustration. What kinds of things do people write in about? You might like to compare these letters with the two parodies from *Viz* on page 55.

Text : *Cosmopolitan* letters

dear cosmo

The naked truth

Thank you for *Naked Male Centre-folds* (July); all were stunning – and very brave. The men had a class and dignity sadly absent from the women in men's magazines.

But how about centrefolds of men that *don't* have perfect looks? I can't be alone in wanting to see men of *all* shapes and sizes stripped to bare essentials. We're always complaining about the flawless women promoted by the media. Let's not sink to the same level.
NC, Essex*

Lenny Kravitz: *Oh my God, Oh my God, Oh my God!!!* Thank you! Thank you! Thank You! From the bottom of my. . .
Sasa Jankovic, Tonbridge, Kent

Safer screening success

Since you published our helpline number in *The Shocking Truth About Cervical Cancer And You* (July) I've had calls from women all over the country – and some from Portugal and the Far East. The main complaints concern the lack of information and support from the medical profession. Some of these women are very distressed and tell stories as horrifying as those you've published. Congratulations on your campaign. Let's hope Frank Dobson takes note and we see some long overdue changes.
Linda Brown, Erewash Voluntary Action CVS
Abnormal Smear Helpline 0115-946 8988

Into the pale

I've just read *The Tan Commandments* (July) about the advantages of sun care lotions. I used to be a 'crash tanner', striving for a deeper tan. I never used a higher factor than SPF4, sometimes used coconut oil and occasionally let myself burn. Now I go for the pale, interesting look, or use self-tanning lotions. I then read *Cosmo's Best Kept Holiday Secrets*, which advised: "Pack a picnic and walk up the beach for a day of calm quiet sunbathing!" After reading *The Tan Commandments*, I'm sure *Cosmo* readers will be prepared with SPF30+ and sun block! **Debbie, Surrey**

Cad, bad and dangerous to know

In *The New Cad* (July) I recognised a familiar breed of man. It took me a number of wounded hearts before I finally admitted such affairs are destructive. I'm now with a sexy man who treats me with genuine respect, and thankfully I can now identify more with the relationships in *What's Sexy Now* (July).
Julia Ford, Bray, Berks

Send your letters for publication to:
Rowena Kenyon, Dear Cosmo, Cosmopolitan, 72 Broadwick Street, London W1V 2BP. *You can also fax her on 0171-439 5016 or e-mail (cosmo.mail@ natmags.co.uk). The writer of the star letter* will win a fabulous Oil of Ulay Cosmetic Box, worth £100. It contains a selection from their Daily Renewal Skincare range, including moisturiser and facewash, plus products from the Colour Cosmetic Collection.*

Text : *Bella* **letters**

Over *to you!*

TIPS... from you
to make life easier

No more tears
Chop and peel onions without crying by keeping them in the fridge — it really does work!
N Mead, Wingrave, Buckinghamshire

Seed sower
If you find small seeds difficult to handle, put them in an empty saccharine dispenser. You then have total control as they come out one by one.
Mrs B Watts, Middlesbrough, Cleveland

Extra soap
Make use of all those small pieces of soap that get left over by putting them in your lavatory cistern. The soap keeps the loo clean and smelling fresh.
Elizabeth Coughlan, Norwich, Norfolk

Bathe in milk
Soften your skin by adding a couple of tablespoons of powdered milk to your bath water — it's cheap, too!
Angela Burns, Whitehaven, Cumbria

Better fit
If you like to wear 10 denier tights but find that they ladder easily, buy a larger size. They'll last much longer as there's more give in them.
Maureen McKenzie, Co Offaly

Hungry seas
On our family holiday this year, my four-year-old nephew, Christopher, was throwing sand into the sea. When his dad asked him what he was doing, he replied: "I'm feeding the sea." A few minutes later, he threw a large stone into the water and again his dad asked him what he was doing. Christopher replied: "That's the sea's pudding!"
Sian Doughty, Ruislip, Middlesex

Sweet dreams
I recently bought some sleeping pills over the counter at my local chemist. I read the leaflet inside and couldn't believe it when it said: 'Side-effects could include nightmares and sleep disturbances'!
It's like taking slimming pills, only to be told that they 'may increase weight'! The whole world's gone absolutely barmy.
Carolyn Whitehead, Yatton, Somerset

Baby for sale
My boyfriend's mum gave birth recently and his young sister, Emma, was beside herself with excitement. We were at the hospital when a midwife popped in and told my boyfriend's mum: "The baby's doing fine and is now eight pounds five."
Emma looked very distressed and shouted: "Please don't sell her, Mum. I love her so much. I've got £10 savings and we can use that." We gently explained that no one was going to take away her new baby sister.
Debbie Waggitt, Gateshead, Tyne & Wear

Spanish dream
We were really excited when our son, David, decided to open a bookshop on the Costa del Sol. Many of our friends thought that he was abandoning us — but far from it. Our lives have been transformed. We go and stay with him for three months in the summer, and again in the winter, and we barely have time to sort out our house before we're off to Spain again. David has made so many friends that we know more people between Malaga and Marbella than we do in our home town. Life has never been better — David's given us the retirement of our dreams!
F Armstrong, Alverstoke, Hampshire

STARletter

Each week the sender of the star letter will receive **£25**

Age discrimination
I heard an old man moaning that his wallet had been stolen with his pension money in it and he assumed that it was some 'young thug'.
I can't believe that the young still get blamed for everything. Last year, I stupidly left my purse in a youth hostel. I was delighted to find that it had been handed in by a teenager, with my £60 still inside. I was extremely lucky, as anyone could have taken my cash — young or old. There are honest and dishonest people in every age group.
Sarah Morgan, Sevenoaks, Kent

Safe sex message
Instead of the Government spending millions of pounds on advertising safe sex, I think it would be a great idea to get certain designers and/or companies to lend their logos and give permission for them to be printed down the side of condoms. I'm sure teenagers would then be proud to wear one!
Yvonne Ayre, Cleveleys, Lancashire

The full monty
A friend went into a shop to buy a Barbie for his daughter. He started chatting to the shop assistant who told him that, for £20, his daughter could have Barbie on a horse; for £25, Barbie in a car and, for £60, Barbie at the hairdressers. Then my friend saw a huge Barbie box for £250 and asked what was in it. The assistant replied: "That's the Barbie gets a divorce from Ken box — in other words, she gets the lot!"
S Baron, Westcliff-on-Sea, Essex

ISN'T LIFE STRANGE?
The pilot of a plane in Germany got a shock when it collided in mid-air — with a rabbit. Investigators believe an eagle dropped its prey while trying to avoid the plane.

PRECIOUS MOMENT
Share a special memory — one you'll never forget

A day to remember
I met Sylvia in 1973 at a disco. I was in the Army. After six weeks, I proposed — she was 18 and I was 21. But her parents gave her an ultimatum, me or them. Sylvia chose me and went to live with my family in London, even though she hadn't met them before.
We had no money and planned a register office wedding, but my brothers arranged a church wedding and paid for a photographer, cake and limousines — it was a wonderful day. It's our 25th wedding anniversary in August and we now have two wonderful daughters and are reconciled with Sylvia's parents.
Terence Fairweather, St Osyth, Essex

Terry and Sylvia's wonderful wedding day

Send us your precious moment in about 200 words, with a photo, to: *Bella*, 25-27 Camden Road, London NW1 9LL. We pay £50 on publication.

Snapshot!
"I've heard of a baby bath, but this is ridiculous"
Debbie Reah, Ditchingham, Suffolk

Each week the sender of the prize photo will receive **£50**

Text : *Men's Health* Letters

LETTERS ▷

I'm all for improving my diet and finding ways of cutting out fat. Your shepherd's pie recipe (*Fat Burner's Bible*, April '98) was a good one, but to cook mince only to let it go cold and then scrape off the fat takes too long. So try this instead:

1. Heat the mince in a frying pan (cook it in its own fat) until it's brown.
2. Meanwhile, boil a kettle. Once the mince is cooked, transfer it to a sieve and pour the kettle of boiling water over the mince. The fat should drain away, leaving lean mince without the wait.
3. Make sure that you run the hot tap in your sink to avoid clogging the drain.

TIM WHITMARSH Chesterfield, Derbyshire

Thanks for your tip, Tim. Have a pen to write your recipes down.

LETTER OF THE MONTH

Short changed

Thanks for the article on ways to survive that weekly curse, the dreaded Monday morning (June '98). It was really helpful, except for one piece of advice which left me more frazzled than ever when I tried to act on it. Professor Howard Weiss suggested looking for money dropped on the pavement which, when found, would put me in a good mood before I reached the office. It doesn't work. Believe me, when you try to look for lost money, you never find it – if you'd given away a free metal detector with the last issue, things might have been different. My suggestion – give money away. Spending a couple of quid on the *Big Issue* is much better for the soul.

J LAST Birmingham

Car wash

For a good aerobic and upper body workout, try washing the car. Having just finished giving mine a good going over – which lasted roughly 45 minutes with me carrying buckets of water, washing and waxing – I reckon I've burnt 600 calories. The action of washing and waxing is also excellent for the deltoid muscles, triceps and biceps. A good workout with a spotless motor... that can't be bad, can it?

GLYN AMOS Saltburn, Cleveland

You couldn't pop round and do our cars Glyn?

Pill talk

I'd like to thank you for your informative article *Up All Night* (June '98) on ways to overcome impotence. What I'd like to know is if I took the new 'impotence-curing' pill Viagra, would it give me a much harder erection?

NAME AND ADDRESS SUPPLIED

The rumours that Viagra can somehow improve a healthy erection are unfounded. According to Dr Harin Padma-Nathan, a leading Viagra researcher in the US: "If you have normal erections, there is no room for improvement with this drug."

Viagra blocks an enzyme that causes erections to wilt, which helps impotent men become hard 'naturally'. If you still attain erections normally, your body chemistry doesn't need the extra help. Taking Viagra may only make your head throb – headaches were reported in about 15 per cent of men who tested the drug.

"Viagra is only for men who have the consistent inability to attain and maintain an erection adequate for sexual performance," Dr Padma-Nathan emphasises.

Watch this space for further developments.

Good stuff

I've never felt compelled to write to a magazine before, until now. What made me put pen to paper were your interviews with the four men who've decided to help others (*The Good Guys*, June '98).

In a our uncaring modern society, it is a refreshing change to hear of four individuals who have unselfishly put aside their own personal problems in an effort to help often desperate people. It moved me to such an extent that I have decided to volunteer for training as a Samaritan.

NAME AND ADDRESS SUPPLIED

MEN'S HEALTH WEBSITE

The *Men's Health* website is now up and running. You can subscribe to your favourite magazine, buy splendid *Men's Health* merchandise, let us know what you think of the magazine as well as check out our sister publications around the globe. All this is now possible via the miracle of the Internet. Check out: **menshealth.com/uk** now!

LET'S HAVE IT!

Send your comments to: **Letters, Men's Health, 7-10 Chandos Street, London W1M 0AD.**
Or you can E-mail your barbs to: **letters@menshealth.co.uk**

Names are withheld on request. Due to the volume of letters we receive we cannot answer letters individually. All correspondence becomes the property of *Men's Health*.

Text : *Bliss* letters

Your letters

Got something you're dying to tell us? Then write to: Your letters, *Bliss*, 3rd Floor, Endeavour House, 189 Shaftesbury Avenue, London WC2H 8JG. Star letter wins a Tea Tree set and all other letters printed get a Tea Tree Cleanser, Toner and Spot Stick, all from Superdrug

superdrug

REACTION ON
'I wanna be on Page Three' in our March issue

* I couldn't believe the Page Three wannabe in your March issue. Who in their right mind would want to flash to the world? She probably wants to do it because she lacks self-confidence and craves attention. Women have fought for years for equal rights to men. It's just so sad that some girls still feel that the only way to get attention is to show off their boobs.
Angry Bliss fan, Bedford

* The Page Three wannabe is fab and has true girl power and strength. She knows what she wants and deserves to do well. A lot of people frown on Page Three models but I respect them and I think they're smart as they use what they've got to make money. As long as they're happy, good luck to them.
Charlotte, Kingston

* This girl's just a big-headed tart. How could anyone be jealous of her? After all, who'd want to go topless in a national newspaper for men to drool over. She's sick in the mind and needs help.
Donna, Scotland

* Rebecca Romain, the girl who stripped to a G-string at the age of 14, should get a life. Doesn't she have anything better to do than strip down in front of greasy, sleazy men? She should concentrate on her schoolwork rather than being a Page Three poser.
A disgusted Leo fan, Lincs

* I'd just like to wish Rebecca loads of luck. I reckon she'll do really well in the future 'cause she's ambitious, confident and optimistic. She's set for success.
Sarah, Cornwall

Bliss tonic
Thanks loads for the *Love Special* which came with the March issue. My mum bought it for me when I was in bed with flu, and it really cheered me up and put me on the road to recovery. The quizzes were great and helped me suss myself out. Please, please hurry up and get your next issue out soon.
Stephanie, Chiswick

All made-up
Our friend reckons all the letters and problems in *Bliss* are made up by the writers and aren't written by the readers, and this is why she doesn't buy it. Please show her that this isn't true by printing this letter. Then she can enjoy *Bliss* as much as we do.
Jess and Em, Liverpool
PS We lurved the love book.
Hope she's convinced now.

Balthazar babe
I've fallen in love with Balthazar – he's just so sweet. All my friends think I'm completely insane so please, please, please print me a pic of him to put in my wallet, then he can be with me all the time.
Kirsty, New Malden

Separated at birth
I was confused by this picture which I found recently in a mag. Is it Mel C or Keith from the Prodigy? I just can't decide so I thought I'd let you work it out.
Carly, West Yorks

Keith Prodigy, Mel C or alien?

Spotted!
I was flicking through an old magazine the other day when I turned the page to see an advert for safe sex with what looked like a piccie of good ol' Sarah Hills from *EastEnders*. She appears a lot younger but it looks like she hasn't changed her clothes for the last few years. Isn't it amazing the things you can get roped into when you're really hard up, eh?
Claire, Birmingham

Sarah's always practised what she preaches

Cool carpet
While I was carpet hunting for my bedroom, I came across a sample named after my fave mag. I decided there and then to go for it. Now my room's truly blissful.
Charlotte, Cambs

Bliss watch

Bliss IB102

Your shout
I'm moaning about how older people treat us. I was waiting for a bus the other day and as it pulled up two old grannies pushed in and nearly shoved me over. If I'd acted like them they would've gone on about how rude the youth of today are. Respect should be given to people of all ages.
Caroline, South Wales

Mate in a million
For friends who are forever

Sally Smith from Birmingham nominates Lesley (right) because she's always listened to her problems in the eight years they've known each other.

Anne Marie Taylor from Bolton nominates Katie (right) because she's her bestest, special mate ever and always will be.

Sarah from Middlesex describes her best mate Toni (right) as her little butterscotch. They're always there for each other and are truly great mates.

Orly from London has a message for her best pal Emma (right), 'Thanks for always being there for me – I'll miss you when you go to Israel.'

14 *b* may

Text : *FHM* letters

LETTERS TO THE EDITOR

Everyone has an opinion. After all, who can forget the wise words of Barry at Primary School, who solemnly swore that babies came out of your mum's arse? And it's exactly this thought process that we salute on the *FHM* Letters page. Tell us anything and everything that's on your mind. From what you thought of the latest issue to the ludicrous price of bread. Far from laughing at you, we'll hand over a nice bottle of Morgan's Spiced Rum. Letter Of The Month gets an entire crate. Send your thoughts to Letters, *FHM*, Mappin House, 4 Winsley Street, London, W1N 7AR. Or e-mail: fhm.letters@ecm.emap.com

Easy life in the world of fiction

Imagine my shock when I discovered that the characters in *EastEnders* only pay £2.50 for *FHM*, while the rest of us humble folk have to fork out £2.80. I was sitting watching the soap when I saw Steve Owen (Martin Kemp) buy the November issue for this new bargain price.
Gavin Robertson, Dundee
Dundee, eh, Gavin? No wonder you're quibbling over a measly 30 pence.

A curious woman writes of her desires

I would honestly like to know just how popular anal sex is for the majority of females. Do they enjoy it, or do they do it solely for the enjoyment of their partner? I regularly enjoy the indulgence of two vibrators and find it very pleasurable to indulge in anal masturbation while being watched. My partner finds this fascinating, but reckons not many men are fortunate enough to come across a woman who thinks like me. I can honestly say I would pay someone to watch me screw myself senseless. Is this common, or am I just being pervy?
Name and address supplied
Strewth! Well readers, does the missus mind a quick trip up the Bourneville Boulevard, or is the Marmite Motorway totally out of bounds? Answers to the usual address please.

I AM NOT AN ANIMAL

"Almost celibate. Balding"
Not only has last month's Animal defied all odds and found a sympathetic woman, this month's candidate has also been unwittingly stitched up by his so-called mates. And yet, amazingly, when we called to let him know of this foul deed, plucky Martin Elsmore was still keen to appear as Animal Number Five. Described by his chums as virtually celibate, the balding hero is also apparently very close to his faithful dog Lucy. "It's all true," he laughs, although there is no mention of the small blind children who have clearly coloured in his tie...
Come on ladies, you don't have to offer to rummage around in his pants, just

Martin Elsmore: "balding hero"

write a nice letter to the poor bugger. Mark your letters Animal Martin, and post them to the address on the left. As for the rest of the nation's mutants, we need a daytime telephone number, plus a recent photograph and a decent whinging letter – mark your envelopes "I Am Not An Animal".

Reader's bird gives game away

With regards to your "Kama Sutra 2" (January 2000), I was astonished that the article finished with the standard male fantasy of one man and two women. My man's fantasy is me, him and another bloke. Why wasn't this suggested?
Name and address supplied
Because it's just plain freaky...

Lard lover questions own sanity

Can I reassure PY of Guildford (Ladies' Ward December 1999) that there are men, like me, who are extremely grateful that

not all women come in the same size and shape. Personally, I find lingerie looks better on women with larger than average attributes. Does that make me abnormal?
Warren Low, via e-mail
Not at all. Big birds in bucket pants. Mmm.

Search for perfect poster

I am looking for pictures of gorgeous girls with their clothes on to decorate my home. They must be amateur models and preferably in black and white. Where can I get such pictures?
Justin, via e-mail
Simple one this, Justin. Buy some black and white film. Step into the street. Take a picture of a woman. Job done.

LETTER OF THE MONTH

Dannii, part one
In your Dannii Minogue interview, she stated that the worst bit of barracking she'd ever had was from two guys sitting in the front row who were completely off their heads. Well I'm one of those guys, and I can honestly say we made her look stupid in front of 200 people in a theatre that can hold 800, and we didn't leave to go to the toilet as she claimed, we headed for the bar. Something that may interest Dannii, however, is that on March 25, I am participating in *West Side Story* at the same theatre. So Dannii, if you want to hear someone sing worse than you, this is your chance.
Adam Howard, Norfolk
Front row at a Dannii Minogue concert. Starring role in West Side Story. Life's just one long party isn't it Adam?

Text : *Viz* letters

(Top Tip, Mr. Teats and Smiles better?, D. Smoog)

Commentary

Text: *Cosmopolitan* reader's letter ('The naked truth'). Here the reader congratulates the magazine on a successful feature and makes a suggestion for improvement. Other letters offer tips, usually concerning domestic activities. This is a tradition in many women's magazines as may be seen by Text: Bella reader's letter. The 'Top Tip' from *Viz*, although funny, is in fact useless.

Sometimes the letters do both these things as demonstrated by Text: *Men's Health* reader's letter ('Letter of the month'). You may be surprised to see a letter in a men's magazine which shares domestic wisdoms. The letters page of *Men's Health* is introduced by the words 'The page where you get to write the words', which is somewhat ironic considering the editorial processes involved. Text: *Bliss* reader's letter ('All made up') acknowledges the general belief that letters are manufactured by the text producers themselves. Even if we take it that the letters are genuine, they are subject to editing since not all letters written to magazines appear in them. Those which do make it have some form of editing. For example, the heading is not the reader's own. It is the text producer who decides which aspect of the letter to highlight and this is usually done in an entertaining manner. In this case it seems deliberately ambiguous – it could to be alluding to the letter writer's Liverpool dialect, 'made-up' is a popular Liverpool phrase to mean 'delighted' or it could refer to the invented nature of readers' letters.

Text: *FHM* reader's letter ('Dannii, part one') has the privileged status of 'letter of the month' and is interesting because it allows the reader a forum for his misogynistic barracking of the Australian celebrity Dannii Minogue. The ideological messages contained in the horoscopes cannot be escaped and the same thing appears to be happening on the letters page. Text: *FHM*'s Dannii, part one contains the message that looking at stereotypically attractive women is a healthy part of male sexuality. This is especially true in the rejoinder 'Front row at a Dannii Minogue concert [. . .] Life's just one long party isn't it Adam?'

The problem page

Magazines are said to problematise aspects of life that can often be solved by purchasing products. Most magazines have a problem page which invites readers to write in with their sexual and emotional dilemmas and problems. Some magazines have both a female and male viewpoint, for example, *More!* has 'Dear Lola' and 'Dear Tony'.

56

How can we examine problem pages from a linguistic viewpoint? For a text to be fully satisfactory to a reader it needs not only the appropriate grammatical links between sentences, **cohesion** (this is explained fully in unit six); but also for the concepts, propositions or events to be related to each other and to be consistent with the overall subject of the text. This semantic and propositional organisation is called **coherence**. Gough and Talbot (1996), following Brown and Yule (1983: 223-4), made a distinction between 'surface' and 'underlying' coherence. Surface coherence refers to the formal linkage properties of texts which is achieved through grammar, and underlying coherence is the point, in the absence of formal links, where the reader accounts for meaning by other methods. This could be by examining the intention of the writer/ speaker or the context in which the utterance takes place. Gough and Talbot believe it is misleading to imagine that coherence can only be achieved in this way. They focused on coherence as the basis for their analysis of a problem page letter which appeared in *The Mirror* newspaper. This letter raises a reader's concern that he may be homosexual because of an experience he had with his best friend when they were both young. The header is 'Guilt over games boys play'. The reader is now married and his friend has a girlfriend. The Agony Aunt's reply reassures the reader that he is 'normal' and, although she does not explicitly state this, she implies that homosexual experiences are a healthy part of growing up as long as they result in confirmed heterosexuality:

> Many heterosexual men have a passing curiosity about homosexuality, and that isn't a bad thing. It compels you to make choices.

As Gough and Talbot point out, there are two explicit cohesive links, 'It' which links back to 'passing curiosity' and also a connection between 'you' and 'many heterosexual men'. 'You' seems to have a dual purpose, referring specifically to the letter writer and generically (referring to a whole class or group, i.e. male heterosexuals). However, in order to make sense of these two sentences, the reader has to rely on their background knowledge by inferring two things. The first is that homosexuality and heterosexuality are separate sexualities. The second is that the letter writer's curiosity about homosexuality is legitimate only in so far as it reaffirms his heterosexuality. It seems he made the 'right' choice on getting married. As may be seen this view is not explicitly stated, rather there are certain points in the reply where the reader has to rely on their knowledge of the social world in order to form a coherent reading of the text.

Activity

With coherence in mind, try examining the Text: Will we end up gay? and the Agony Aunt's reply to see whether there are any points where you have to use your knowledge of the world.

Commentary

The header 'Will we end up gay?' summarises the gist of the 'problem' (note that it is not a direct quotation from the letter). As Gough and Talbot found, the Agony Aunt's response reassures the reader of the 'normality' of her worries, she establishes herself as 'analyst' and a solution to the 'problem' is proposed. The reply is regulatory in that it confirms the acceptability of certain types of behaviour:

> and if you do decide you are gay, that's OK ... Time will show whether you prefer boys or girls – some people end up fancying both and that's OK too.

The message certainly appears to be quite liberal. However, following an adversative clause which is introduced by 'but', the teenage reader is hardly likely to want to be different to the 'vast majority':

> But the vast majority of these teenagers don't go on to be gay.

'But' signals to the reader that what the Agony Aunt has said previously is going to be revised in some way. This, together with the advice to approach some boys, tends to reaffirm the 'naturalness' of heterosexuality. The 'when' clause:

> So, when we first get interested in sex, it's common for people to turn to close friends

leads on to the taken for grantedness of the assumption 'as the opposite sex is too scary to approach'. The suggestion that there is something scary about the opposite sex has the effect of helping to polarise the sexes. In order to make sense of this statement the reader has to make the connection with a stereotyped view of sexual relationships from her knowledge of the world. In order to understand how males might be perceived as 'scary', she must infer that they are somehow predators and that females are victims in sexual encounters. This commonsense view

Text : Will we end up gay?

Will we end up gay?

A year ago, my friend and I started kissing and touching each other intimately. We still do it, although we think about boys all the time. Will we be gay when we're older, or just mixed up? I know people who are screwed up about similar experiences.
Ashamed 13-year-old

Lots of teenagers worry that gay fantasies or experiences mean they'll be gay forever. They don't. When we're young, most of our time is spent with same sex friends. So, when we first get interested in sex, it's common for people to turn to close friends, as the opposite sex is too scary to approach. But the vast majority of these teenagers don't go on to be gay. Instead of sticking a label on yourself now, take some time to work out your feelings and if you do decide you are gay, that's OK. In the meantime, you've said that you and your friend fancy boys, so perhaps it's time to approach some. Time will show whether you prefer boys or girls – some people end up fancying both and that's OK too.

accords with the dominant discourse and in carrying out the necessary inferencing work the reader is constructing for herself a particular subject position. The construction of subject positions is explained in Unit five. As was the case with *The Mirror* Agony Aunt's reply, on the surface the message is quite liberal, there are no homophobic views explicitly stated, rather these are set up in such a way that it is the reader who has to supply the missing links in order to make sense of the texts.

Note that the topic of homosexuality is usually covered on the problem pages which upholds a general view of it as deviant behaviour.

Magazine narratives: readers' true stories

The 'bitty' nature of magazines due to the mixing of genres on the same page was mentioned in unit three. Text: 'Don't become a mum by mistake', from *Sugar*, purports to be a reader's letter to other readers but as it unfolds it becomes more like a narrative, therefore lending itself to an analysis as such a form. There is a diary type extract which gives details of a typical day in the life of a young mother and also a 'help box' with information for readers who may be worried that they are pregnant. Text producers and readers have certain expectations of genres. For example, normally there would not be a header or subheadings accompanying a letter, rather this is a convention we have come to expect of magazines.

Theorists have identified rules for the construction of narratives. These help with the organisation and help to explain why narratives are recognised as such. Carter and Nash (1990) refer to three main structural units which are agreed to be fundamental to narrative organisation. These can be split into macro-units and micro-units:

Macro-units	Micro-units
Setting:	in which specific linguistic structures mark time, place and other circumstances, including the 'characters' of participants.
Complication	in which specific linguistic structures, most markedly *tense*, define the basic episodes in
Resolution	the story and their final 'resolution' or denouement.
Moral	in which elements crucial to the telling of the tale are encoded. Here linguistic structures determine the 'point' or 'purpose' of the story.

Deviations to these 'rules' can occur, for example some texts open mid-action:

> 'It's a twenty-footer.'
> 'Twenty-five. All three tons of him.'

The effect produced, due to an absence of orientation, makes the reader feel as though they are chance observers of some action.

Activity

Can you identify the structural units in Text: 'Don't become a mum by mistake'? Use the headings suggested by Carter and Nash.

Commentary

Setting
The narrative follows a conventional patterning in relation to time orientation:

> 'One morning, three months after I'd first had sex ... soon I was throwing up every day. When, days later ...'

The reader is taken step by step through a sequence of events.

Place
It is not implicitly stated but it can be inferred that the story begins at home. The reader is guided from one location to another which include:

> doctor's surgery,
> hospital,
> home (for a meeting with boyfriend),
> school (when the storyteller recounts her unhappy treatment there due to her pregnancy).

The story continues with the birth, which begins at home but takes place in the hospital, then after the birth a return to school, leaving school and another visit to the doctors.

Complication
Events are narrated chronologically:

Sugar real life

"don't become a mum by

Many girls may *think* they're ready to have sex, but some make the decision too quickly.

Dianne: "I love my son but I'll always miss being a teenager."

(*Above*) Shoes, toys, teddies... it's an expensive business being a parent.

Remember: it's illegal to have sex if you're under 16, and it's always best to

mistake"

SEX AND YOU

Dianne Longman, 16, is one girl who lived to regret it. Here is her letter to you...

Dear Sugar readers
I'm writing to you, not because I need to get things off my chest, but 'cause I don't want you to end up like me. I was 15 when I got pregnant. I met Martin at school when I was 14, and we just clicked – we were both virgins, but decided to lose our virginity to one another. I'd learnt about contraception in school, so we always used a condom. But to be honest, we were never sure if it was on properly...

One morning, three months after I'd first had sex, I woke up feeling really sick. Soon I was throwing up every day. When, days later, I still wasn't better, Mum took me to the doctor for a blood test. Nothing could've prepared me for the news a few days later. I walked into the surgery alone.
"You're not ill," said the doctor. "You're pregnant. We'll do a scan to make sure."
"But my periods are so irregular – I haven't had one for almost a year!" I insisted.
Gently, she explained that when you're a teenager, hormone levels can sometimes be enough to release an egg but not enough to bleed. I froze on the spot.
"Please don't tell Mum," I begged. "Not until we're *totally* sure."
Thankfully she agreed.
"I've got to have an ovarian scan," I told Mum and Dad in the waiting room. "I'm going to the hospital this afternoon."
By 3pm, I was looking at *my* baby on a monitor screen. I was *terrified!* When I saw the tiny heartbeat, I broke down. I knew I couldn't have an abortion, but how could I tell everyone?
As soon as I got home and saw Mum, I couldn't keep quiet.
"I'm pregnant!" I blurted out.
"I had a feeling you were," she said, hugging me close. She couldn't have been more understanding.

That night, Martin came over and we talked for hours. He was gobsmacked, but pleased. I was so relieved, 'cause I was afraid he'd go mad.
The rest of the pregnancy passed quickly. The hardest thing was going to school. I had to wear this huge maternity dress and people were so cruel, calling me a slag – it was awful. But bitchy remarks were the last thing on my mind when I got my first contraction on the morning of July 19. It was *agony*.
"Hold on, love!" yelled my mum, while Martin and Dad got ready to drive to the hospital.
Two hours later, I gave birth to Kyle. The next few days passed in a blur, with visitors arriving to congratulate me... but then it all stopped and I was alone. Can you imagine how I felt?
Once I was home, Mum showed me how to change nappies and mix formula and Martin came round to help, but it was me who got up in the night when Kyle cried. It was exhausting.
Two months later, I went back to school, but I was so tired that I couldn't concentrate. I had been expected to get A and B grade GCSEs and I'd had such big plans for my future, but with Kyle, I couldn't cope. I had to leave.

My friends started drifting away. I just couldn't relate to them anymore. While they talked about boys and make-up, all I could talk about was the price of nappies. I became really depressed and soon I was crying all the time. The tiniest things set me off; a tiff with Martin, even a sad episode of *Neighbours*. Mum persuaded me to go to the doctor.
"These feelings are very common," he explained. "Lots of new mothers go through it."
He prescribed anti-depressants and, thankfully, they worked. Within a couple of months I was feeling loads better.
Me and Martin got a council flat together at Easter which helped. But there's so much pressure on our relationship to work, much more than there is for most couples our age; I couldn't just finish it without a thought for Kyle. Luckily, Martin and I are closer than ever, but I hate the fact that we don't have any freedom. We can't just go off partying with our mates like you probably can. It feels as if we miss out on so much.
I'm far happier now and I'm off the anti-depressants, but I still get sad and lonely. Martin works in his family's café every day to support us and when he gets in at night he's so exhausted he just goes to bed, so I hardly ever see him.
It's a struggle financially, too – we have to spend every penny on Kyle and the flat. I can't remember the last time I bought myself anything. My Saturdays in Miss Selfridge are long gone.
If you're considering having sex, please wait 'til you're *totally* ready and know you could cope with whatever happens. If you *do* decide to sleep with someone, you've got to use a condom, and you've got to make sure you're using it properly. But be aware that no contraception is 100% safe. Unless you fancy having no money and no life, don't risk getting pregnant or you could spend the rest of your life regretting it. Of course I love my son, but I'll always miss being a teenager.
love Diane xxxxx

my typical day

7am Wake up to Kyle crying at full volume.
7.30am Give him breakfast, dress him, then 'play'.
9am Put him back to bed.
11am Kyle wakes again and we play before doing the shopping and visiting Mum.
3.45pm Return home and put Kyle to bed before

cooking his tea and doing the washing and Hoovering.
4pm Martin comes home.
5.30pm Kyle has his tea.
8pm Put Kyle to bed and cook dinner for me and Martin before washing up and going to bed, hoping Kyle will stay asleep until it all starts again.

help box

If you're worried you may be pregnant, don't ignore the problem, but try not to panic. First, find out for sure. Ask for a test at your local Brook Advisory Centre, Family Planning Clinic (find them in the phone book) or ask your GP. If the result *is* positive, they'll give you all the help and advice you need.

wait until you're in a loving relationship and 100% sure you're ready.

Sugar 79

Interview: Kate Thompson, Solent News. Photos: Tim Roney.

63

the narrator's feelings of sickness, discovery of pregnancy, viewing her baby on a monitor, informing parents and boyfriend of the pregnancy, enduring cruel remarks from schoolfriends.

Giving birth, being overwhelmed by visitors, then feelings of lost elation. She experiences difficulty coping, sleepless nights, having to leave school, losing friends.

Resolution

Seeing the doctor and being prescribed tranquilisers, getting a flat, being closer to boyfriend, coming off tranquilisers.

Moral

The message conveyed is that it is better to hold off from having sex: 'If you're considering having sex, please wait 'til you're *totally* ready and know you could cope with whatever happens.' This supports the direct imperative in the title 'Don't become a mum by mistake.' However, the storyteller warns the reader: 'If you *do* decide to sleep with someone you've got to use a condom, and you've got to make sure you're using it properly.' Within the wider context, the story is from a sixteen-page sex special, the message accords with the ideology of the magazine which is explicitly stated in a message at the bottom of each page: 'Remember: it's illegal to have sex if you're under l6, and it's always best to wait until you're in a loving relationship and 100% sure you're ready.'

Dialogue within the text

There are samples of dialogue within the text which it might be useful to examine in terms of function. Carter and Nash (1990) refer to three functions of dialogue in narratives:

1   To interrupt the flow of general narration, slow down the movement of the story, and concentrate attention on a particular event, relationship, etc.
2   To bring out character, and relationships between characters; personalities being revealed by what they say, what others say to or about them, and how they respond to what others say.
3   To create the sense of a background by supplying impressions - conveyed through personal interactions - of a society, its manners, its concerns, its material objects.

The purpose of the dialogue in Text: 'Don't become a mum by mistake', does concentrate attention on particular events. For example, the sequence at the doctor's seems designed to emphasise the enormity of the news:

> 'You're not ill,' said the doctor. 'You're pregnant. We'll do a scan to make sure.'
> 'But my periods are so irregular – I haven't had one for almost a year!' I insisted.
> [...]
> 'Please don't tell Mum,' I begged. 'Not until we're *totally* sure.'

The style of reporting – 'I insisted' and 'I begged' – gives the reader an indication of the storyteller's state of mind.

There is also a one-sided extract, the storyteller to her parents:

> 'I've got to have an ovarian scan,' I told Mum and Dad in the waiting room. 'I'm going to the hospital this afternoon.'

This seems designed to provide some background.

The next sequence is related to characterisation and the relationship between parent and child:

> 'I'm pregnant!' I blurted out.
> 'I had a feeling you were,' she said, hugging me close. She couldn't have been more understanding.
> [...]
> 'Hold on, love!' yelled my mum....

If we look at the verb tenses it can be seen that there is a clear sequence. Indeed, a characteristic of narratives is that they are in the past tense, since they recount events which have happened and this narrative is no exception. However, this does change towards the end of the story when events move into the present: 'But there **is** so much pressure on our relationship....' Since the text appears to be a cautionary tale to the magazine's young readers, it could be that bringing the story into the present has the effect of making it more immediate and relevant.

The storyteller breaks the narrative frame at various points in the story when there is a change of address form to appeal directly to the reader:

Can you imagine how I felt?...
We can't just go off partying with our mates like you probably can....
If you're considering having sex....

This direct form fits in with the idea of the story as a personal letter and appears designed to trigger feelings of empathy within the reader. The same could be said of the large visual image accompanying the story which is of the storyteller looking directly at the reader. Typography is used to suggest intonation and stress which would occur in naturally occurring speech:

'Not until we're *totally* sure.'...
I was looking at *my* baby on a monitor screen....
I was *terrified*!

There are one or two clichéd expressions such as 'I froze on the spot' which indicates the youthfulness and naivety of the storyteller. Clichés are society's well-worn expressions which, through over-use, have lost their effect.

Extension

Can you identify these patterns of narrative in other stories in magazines?

Summary

An examination of the contents of magazines revealed that **ideological** messages permeate the various texts. Often these messages are contradictory, for example in *Bliss*, the young reader was reassured that her gay fantasies were 'OK' which is quite a liberal message even by today's standards. Yet, other messages, for example those contained in the horoscope, addressed the reader as though she was already in a relationship with a boy, which accords with the dominant ideology.

Who am I?
The relationship between the text producer and interpreter

This unit will consider the relationship between the text producer and interpreter by examining the *identity* of the writer and the *subject positions* constructed for readers. The role of the reader in taking up or resisting the subject positions on offer will also be considered.

Magazine discourse, since it is written, is a monologue because the producer of the text and the interpreter are remote from each other at the time of writing. Writers of magazines are in difficulty in addressing a mass audience. They cannot possibly claim to know the identity of each individual reader, yet they often speak as though they already know the reader, their thoughts, attitudes, likes and dislikes. In order to do this an imaginary addressee is constructed which I will refer to as the *ideal-reader*, but you may come across other terms for this.

Talbot (1992) focuses in particular on how teenage girls' magazines contribute to the construction of femininity. In order to illustrate this she examines the 'population' of the text, the 'tissue of voices' made up of the writer, reader and various other characters. For the purpose of this book the range of textual features suggested by Talbot will be used to explore the construction of subject positions for the text producer and reader.

Constructing subject positions

The compensatory tendency when addressing audiences en masse is known as **synthetic personalisation** (Fairclough 1989). This has the effect of creating the impression that the writer knows the reader personally. One of the techniques employed in order to achieve this is the simulation of two-way conversation:

Text : Childbirth? Ironing? That's *Nothing*!

> Tired of hearing the missus moan about 'women's problems'? Course you are. That's why we decided to test the validity of their claim that … sometimes it's hard to be a woman.
>
> (*FHM* February 1997)

In conversational analysis there is a set of utterances known as *adjacency pairs* because they usually go together, for example a question will usually demand an answer. In the above exchange, since the reader is not present, they are unable to supply the answer. Nevertheless the text producer proceeds as though the reader has said 'Yes, I am tired of hearing the missus moan about women's problems.' This technique has the effect of drawing the reader in by causing them to interact with the text in considering what the question entails, even though they are unlikely to respond aloud.

In Text: 'Childbirth? Ironing? That's *Nothing*!' another feature of conversation is achieved by the use of dots to indicate a pause. Here the text producer heightens the reader's anticipation as to what is coming next just as a dramatic pause would in real conversation:

That's why we decided to test the validity of their claim that …

The ideal-reader

The use of pronouns is also a way in which text producers create a relationship with the reader. By using the pronoun 'you', which covers anyone who reads the text, the text producer appears to address the reader directly.

Text : Six simple secrets to keep you looking fabulous

> You can have a flat tummy, healthy hair, a glowing complexion and lovely make-up by following our golden beauty rules.
>
> (*Bella* August 1998)

The subject position of the reader is someone who has said 'I can't possibly have a flat tummy....' The modal auxiliary 'can' is emphatic in reassuring a doubtful imaginary addressee.

Another way in which text producers imply that they know the reader is by the use of **presupposition**:

> You don't have to feel like crap every time you get your period. Check out these ways to beat the blues....

This presupposes that you (the implied reader) do feel like 'crap' every time you get your period. Presuppositions are taken-for-granted assumptions. The text producer refers to something as though it already exists, with which the reader is invited to identify. In the act of doing so the reader is constructing herself as a member of a community of women for whom periods are a source of misery.

The identity of the text producer

The text producers of magazines must also construct an identity for themselves. The writer's subject position, as the reader's, is not fixed but may change, even within the same text. The writer can simultaneously be the reader's friend, adviser and entertainer, or their identity can shift between these roles.

It is not always clear whether texts are singly or multiply authored since the writer's use of 'I' or 'we' is not always a reliable clue to their identity, but writers do make interesting use of the pronoun 'we'. This may be *inclusive*:

Text : A Man For All Reasons

He's almost perfect. If he wasn't, you wouldn't be seeing him. That said, even almost-perfect men behave in ways that make you want to scream, shout, bellow, cry, rage and roar: 'Stop that! I'm sick of it! You're making me hate you!' Indeed, **we've** all tried that tactic, but for some reason it doesn't work. [my emphasis.]

(*Cosmopolitan* September 1998)

Here the text producer includes the reader, who is expected to recognise themselves as a member of a community of women who have at some time been in the frustrating scenario outlined. The writer also belongs to this universal group of women.

The pronoun 'we' can also be used in its *exclusive* sense to distance the reader as in Text: 'Childbirth? Ironing? That's *Nothing*!': 'That's why **we** decided to test the validity of their claim that....' Here 'we' refers to the text producer and her colleagues. When magazine text producers wish to claim authority or expert status, they often invoke the weight of the rest of the editorial team to endorse what they are saying. Part of the text producer's identity can be established by examining the degree of certainty attached to her assertions. This is referred to as **modality**. There are nine **modal auxiliary verbs**: 'can', 'may', 'could', 'must', 'might', 'shall', 'should', 'will' and 'would'. These verbs help the main verb to express a range of moods such as doubt, ability, possibility and obligation. Take a look at the following utterances:

A: I **will** come to your party.
B: I **may** come to your party.

Which speaker would you expect to see at your party?

In the following example from the teenage magazine *It's Bliss*, the modal auxiliary verb 'can' indicates the writer's high degree of commitment to the assertion that condoms are a way of reducing the risk of contracting HIV.

Text : 'The ultimate sex checklist'

> When used correctly, a condom can reduce the risk of contracting HIV – the virus that causes AIDS – to almost zero.
>
> (*It's Bliss* July 1996)

If the modal auxiliary were more cautious, e.g. 'a condom **may** reduce the risk', this would be less commanding and the reader is likely to lose confidence in the reliability of the text producer and indeed the efficacy of condoms.

Another way of examining the text producer's identity is to look at the way she reports the words of others. Does she signal agreement or does she distance herself?

Text : 'Bread winners'

> HISTORY HAS BEEN KIND TO JOHN MONTAGU. HERE WAS A MAN whose first noticeable act on becoming Lord Commissioner of the Admiralty, in December 1744, was to move both his wife and his mistress into his official residence. He then sired four illegitimate children by the latter, before she was murdered in mysterious circumstances. After that, he brought one of his greatest friends to trial on trumped-up charges and throughout all this, he still found time to lead the British navy to its 'lowest depths of inefficiency and corruption'.
>
> (*GQ Active* September 1998)

In Text: 'Bread winners', the identity of the person quoted is not stated but the text producer uses the quote in support of a damning character sketch from which she can disassociate herself if necessary. In the same text the writer appears to be in agreement:

71

From a health point of view, the merits of sandwiches are diverse; they can be as good or as bad for you as you like. 'Avoid pate, mayonnaise, and cheese in sandwiches because of the fat content,' says Lisa Piearce of the Sports Nutrition Service, advisor to the England rugby team and the Football Association.

The reporting verb 'says' indicates that someone else is responsible for the utterance, in this case a nutritional expert. The quotation is used to support earlier views of the writer in favour of healthy eating.

Some utterances are incorporated in single quotation marks which Fairclough (1989) refers to as **scare quotes**. Scare quotes can signal that there is something wrong with the expression or simply that it belongs to someone else.

Text : The ultimate sex checklist

Sure, skipping the odd brekkie, scoffing an extra bar of chocolate and 'forgetting' your PE kit to get out of gym may seem harmless enough, but it's all those tiny lapses which can make the diffference between looking good and looking like you're suffering.

(*Bliss* July 1996)

Since 'forgetting' is in scare quotes it signals that this is a deliberate action but to make sense of this we need to do some **inferencing** work. We need to draw on our existing knowledge of the world to come up with a reason why young women might 'forget' their PE kit. Presumably this is because they do not want to do PE when menstruating. This view is presented as **common sense** and likely to relate to the experience of many women, but when subject to scrutiny there is nothing 'natural' about the practice, rather it is culturally constructed. Ironically, many current advertisements for sanitary towels and tampons actually construct a subject who engages in physical activities, e.g. skateboarding when menstruating (see Mills 1997: 12). The following reference from the same text seems to acknowledge such adverts.

OK – so there's nothing you **can't** do when you've got your period. . . .

[emphasis as in the original text]

When writers make reference to other, prior texts, as in the above example, this is known as intertextuality.

Scare quotes can also be used as a way of endorsing an expression, which is possibly the case with the next example from Text: 'The ultimate sex checklist':

So before you decide to 'do it', give yourself the third degree with this questionnaire. . . .

Here the words 'do it' are likely to be a **euphemism** for sexual intercourse which the text producer believes the implied reader to be familiar with. Euphemisms are a polite way of avoiding embarrassment by indirectly referring to topics which are taboo in society.

The relationship between the text producer and reader

Text producers often mimic the speech patterns of the implied reader with a view to establishing common ground between them. The following examples are from 'The ultimate sex checklist' previously referred to – 'serious fast forward', 'flip out', 'freak out', 'mega make-out session'. Fairclough (1991) refers to informal styles as the 'discourse of the life-world', in other words the language of ordinary life. This can be contrasted with 'official discourse' which is more formal. Within the same text there can be a mixture of both discourses. In Text: 'The ultimate sex checklist', dealing with the topic of safe sex, the official, formal term 'condom' is used on one page and the unofficial, less formal term 'love glove' is used on the next to refer to the same item. This mixture of discourses creates an air of credibility which at the same time is less authoritarian in tone.

From the magazines examined in this unit it can be seen that the relationship between the text producer and the reader has been one of informality and friendship. In minimising the social distance between them, the text producer is in a powerful position to mould a like-minded reader. The relationship, however, is not symmetrical – it is always the text producer who has the authority to command the reader to do things and never the otherway round:

73

Text : The ultimate sex checklist

> Hold the sex!
> Don't even think about saying yes to him until you've said yes to these eight questions!
>
> (*It's Bliss* July 1996)

It is the text producer who supplies the knowledge which the reader is thought to be in need of:

Text : Late summer colour

> Late summer seems to be the time when some of the freshness has gone from the garden and the plants can, quite frankly, look a little bit tired.
> So, in this issue, I'll be introducing you to some real stars which will bloom right on into autumn and I'll also give you some simple ideas on how to revamp a boring patio with decking and beautiful plants.
>
> (*Bella* 25 August 1998)

The editorial

Many magazines contain a letter from the editor to readers. The purpose of the editorial is to introduce the magazine's contents, but it also gives the text producers the opportunity to address their readers directly. The reader synthesised is someone who is thought to share the same views, attitudes and beliefs as the text producer. The length of editorials varies as may be seen from Texts: 'From the editor' and 'Editor's Letter'. The editor's letter has its own particular style which corresponds to the style of the magazine.

from the editor

e at *Cosmo* pride ourselves on bringing you the information and inspiration you won't find in any other women's magazine, which is why 26 years after our launch, we're still the best selling young women's magazine in Britain. And we know from your letters you can't get enough of our unique insights into men; not only what makes them tick, but all their deep-rooted idiosyncrasies. That's why, this month, we've devoted eight pages to the mysterious world of men. We cajoled the best and the bravest male writers to divulge the kind of information they would never spill to any other publication. And I'm delighted to announce their secrets make eye-opening, provoking reading. Instead of the usual mag-stuff, like why men watch porn (which, d-u-u-r-r-r, doesn't take a genius to figure out), Ben Edison delves deeper and explains why your man wants you to watch porn *with* him. Rather than another article on why men fear commitment, Phil Robinson divulges the secret psyche of the single man. And if you're convinced what a man really wants for his birthday involves lots of tongues, don't go anywhere near him until you've read Roland White's wonderful piece on page 92.

On the subject of men and tongues, *Cosmo* reveals the sex secret of the year that, once mastered, guarantees to make him yours for ever (if, of course, that's what you want). And guess what? It only takes five seconds and not a single scented candle in sight! Find the details on page 153 – and please let us know how it transforms your sex life.

All that said, a growing number of women don't want to be bothered with the time-consuming business of understanding the male mind. Many women today are quite happy, thank you, to have male company to carry their luggage through airports, give them a mind-blowing orgasm, escort them to fabulous black tie parties, put up a shelf (which of course they *could* do but, hey, life's too short) or just accompany them to the pub, but as for the sexual politics. . . forget it. On the strength of this, our feature entitled *A Man For All Reasons* (page 58) makes compelling reading. Oh, and don't forget to jot down the telephone numbers and e-mail addresses we've generously given at the end of the article.

As September is the big fashion month of the new season, we're delighted to bring you a comprehensive, new style round-up, with a bumper 37 pages of fabulous clothes you'll *want* to wear. We're also thrilled to offer every *Cosmo* reader a 10 per cent exclusive discount at Dorothy Perkins for your, inevitable, forthcoming shopping sprees.

And to add to the most enticing magazine package on the shelves this month is a wonderful, free beauty magazine in association with our friends at Oil of Ulay, called *Great Skin, Hair and Make-up at 20, 30, 40.* Featuring everything you need to know to guarantee good looks now, and 10 years from now, it's truly indispensable.

Now here's a tip: make sure you reserve your copy of October *Cosmo* when we'll be giving away free to every reader *The Cosmopolitan Bedside Book Of Orgasms.* Excited? You will be. See you then! □

Text : *FHM* editor's letter

EDITOR'S LETTER

When I was growing up in the Seventies, local ruffians would spend their spare time annoying ordinary folk with what, in hindsight, has to be viewed as fairly mundane teenage trouble-making. These apprentice criminals would get their kicks by throwing conkers at passing cars, pushing flaming dog turds through people's letterboxes, scrumping or even standing on opposing sides of the street ready to scare passing motorcyclists by hoisting up imaginary ropes. Wickedness such as mugging and vandalism was reserved solely for the boys from the orphanage or the very roughest council estate. Yet now, not a day goes by without a newspaper reporting yet another heinous crime commited by a career criminal whose testes have yet to see the outside of his body. These aren't just bored young scrotes with mischief on their minds; no, these miscreants are a new breed of psychopathic little runt who like nothing more than a weekend of outrunning the local constabulary in high performance motor vehicles and setting fire to old folk. Annoyingly, the authorities are powerless to do anything about them until they grow old enough to be chucked in jail. Read about their exploits in our "Britain's Scariest Kids" feature (which starts on page 106). And, seeing as you never know when you're going to be confronted by pre-pubescent hooligans, you should take special notice of the section on subduing a pint-sized assailant. You might just save yourself an embarrassing beating.

If any of these evil kids were to bump into one or other of our collection of amazing grandads ("To Hell And Back", page 126) they might think twice before "having a go". Our heroic silvertops survived everything that World War II could throw at them: blanket bombings, seas of fire, prisoner of war camps and trench warfare. One of them, Bertrand "Jimmy" James is even a genuine survivor of the Great Escape. Perhaps we should give our legendary wrinklies back their Tommy-guns and let them mete out a little old-fashioned discipline?

Enjoy the issue!

Anthony Noguera
EDITOR

Activity

'From the editor' and 'Editor's Letter' are editorials from two different magazines. Can you identify the subject position of the implied reader? How is language used to mediate the relationship between the text producer and reader? The following questions, adapted from Talbot (1992), may help:

76

- ◎ Who is speaking to whom? What pronouns are used?
- ◎ What identity(ies) does the text producer construct for themselves? Look at modality — is she confident or hesitant in what she says?
- ◎ What assumptions does the text producer make about the reader? Are there common-sense views which the reader is presumed to share?
- ◎ Who does she think the reader is? Are there any presuppositions, e.g. claims about the reader which the text producer could not possibly know?
- ◎ Is the text producer being friendly? Are conversational features used such as adjacency pairs?

Commentary

It can be seen even from the header that each letter has a distinctive style. The *Cosmopolitan* text begins 'From the editor' which is actually a designation (signing off). If the reader wished to be difficult she could ask 'What from the editor?' Presumably the motive for putting it this way is to sound caring, as though the reader is being given something. The *FHM* heading is more matter-of-fact: 'Editor's letter.' The editor of *Cosmopolitan* speaks on behalf of the production team using the pronoun 'we'. She attempts to make herself and the team more familiar to the reader by abbreviating the title to 'Cosmo'. In contrast the editor of *FHM* speaks to the reader in the first person singular but changes address form to include the rest of the team when he talks about the contents of the magazine.

In *Cosmopolitan* there are conversational features: 'And guess what?' Also exclamations: 'Oh, and don't forget...' The editor also emulates the latest in-group sounds — 'd-u-u-r-r-r' (used to signal something obvious) — to show that she is on the same wavelength as the reader. The editor of *FHM* also chooses lexis which is likely to be used by the implied reader: 'scrotes' and 'runt'. The meaning of 'runt' in this context is clearly not 'the smallest and weakest young animal in a litter'. There are also conversational features. 'These aren't just bored young scrotes with mischief on their minds; no, these miscreants are a new breed of psychopathic little runt ...' 'No' is used for emphasis in informal conversation. Characters are given nicknames, 'heroic silvertops', Bertrand "Jimmy" James and legendary wrinklies', to make these figures sound more familiar to the reader.

77

The tone of the *Cosmopolitan* letter is self-congratulatory concerning the success of the magazine's formula and incorporates the readers' apparent satisfaction with the magazine by referring to letters which they send in. The *FHM* letter is a first person narrative account of the editor's childhood. The tone of the letter is one of self-mocking irony as he recounts the male juvenile pastimes of 'throwing conkers at passing cars' and 'pushing flaming turds through people's letterboxes', which of course the reader will recognise as 'harmless' fun.

The ideal reader of *Cosmopolitan* is a young woman who is heterosexual. We know that she is a young woman because this is explicitly stated:

> we're still the best selling young women's magazine in Britain.

It is presupposed that the reader is in a heterosexual, monogomous relationship:

> Ben Edison delves deeper and explains why your man wants you to watch porn with him.

The reader is presumed to share the magazine's preoccupation with men:

> you can't get enough of our unique insights into men.

The reader is the novice who does not understand 'the mysterious world of men' and the text producer is the expert who is in a position to enlighten her. The text sets up opposition between the sexes but also acknowledges changes taking place in society:

> a growing number of women don't want to be bothered with the time consuming business of understanding the male mind. . . .

The ideological messages of texts will be considered in more detail in Units six and seven.

The ideal reader of *FHM* is able to infer that there is a stigma attached to being male and being beaten by someone younger and smaller than themselves. We know that it is a male who is addressed:

> And, seeing as you never know when you're going to be confronted by pre-pubescent hooligans, you should take special notice of the section on subduing a pint-sized assailant. You might just save yourself an embarrassing beating.

since women in our society are not expected to nor indeed encouraged to fight.

Although the reader will already have purchased the magazine, both editors go to great lengths to persuade the reader that their magazine is better than its rivals. The *Cosmopolitan* editor refers to *seeing* the reader whereas the *FHM* editor compels the reader to 'enjoy the issue!' Both letters are personally signed. The photographs accompanying the letters add to the personal touch but differ in that Anthony Noguera looks directly into the camera with a slightly bemused expression. Mandi Norwood gazes off into the distance, smiling. Despite their different styles it is likely that both letters are effective in establishing a relationship with their respective readers.

Resisting subject positions

In any textual analysis it is important to consider the role of the reader in taking up or resisting the subject positions on offer. For some readers this would be extremely easy, for example, a woman reader would recognise instantly that an utterance such as 'Tired of hearing the missus moan about "women's problems"?' is not addressing her. An adult, heterosexual male, on the other hand, would have no such difficulty even though he may not be in agreement.

Elizabeth Frazer (1997) found from her analysis of the transcripts of girls discussing *Jackie* magazine that they 'strongly suggest that a self-conscious and reflexive approach to texts is a natural approach for teen-age girls'. We all bring our own particular 'baggage' to an interpretation of a text, which may be influenced by our age, sex, class, ethnicity and race. In analysing texts the notion that there is one valid and unitary meaning of a text ought to be critiqued. The unequal relationship between the text producer and reader has been highlighted but it must be remembered that the reader is the one who is ultimately in control since she can stop reading at any time and can switch loyalty from one magazine to another at whim.

Extension

You might like to carry out your own analysis of a text then ask a fellow student to analyse the same text and compare them. It is unlikely that you both will come up with exactly the same interpretation. In your comparison what points did you have in common? What differences emerged?

Summary

There are a range of techniques which writers use to engage with the reader in constructing subject positions for themselves and the reader. In this unit we have looked at pronouns, conversational features, presupposition, common sense and modality. These are not the only ones available but some of the most commonly used.

Unit **six**

The discourse of magazines

Aim of this unit

The aim of this unit is to explore some of the linguistic devices which enable whole passages from magazines to work in meaningful ways. This will involve analysing the way language features work across the boundaries of single sentences to form whole texts.

Magazines are regarded as quite 'bitty' texts yet this does not pose a problem for the reader because, generally, there is a coherence present which is achieved in several ways. Before outlining what these are, it would be helpful to explain how the term **discourse** will be used in this unit.

Discourse

Mills (1997) explains the complicated history of the term and how it is used in different ways by a number of disciplines, e.g. linguistics, psychology and literature. For the purpose of this unit, discourse will be used in two ways. First, in relation to extended stretches of language, whether written or spoken, discourse is used to refer to the internal organisation of the text which gives it coherence. To get a sense of how the text is organised it can be useful to look at cohesive ties, some of which will be outlined below.

81

Linguistic determinism: ideological viewpoints

The second sense in which the term will be used is in relation to the ideological stance taken by the text producer. The Sapir-Whorf hypothesis suggests that the language we speak may influence or determine the way we perceive the world. The text producers of magazines present a particular view of the world as they see it and attempt to get others to see it that way too. We also talk about discourses in relation to specific social institutions, e.g. the discourse of education. What this is referring to is the way certain areas of social life, in this case education, produce utterances and practices which have particular meanings in relation to the context of the institution. For example, the practice of grading pupils according to their ability just seems to make good sense and is rarely questioned. This is something which has developed within education and is therefore socially constructed. In this unit we will consider the discourse of magazines both in relation to the organisation of the text and the practices of text producers.

Text

Text is a term which has been used throughout the book without explanation, so it might be a good idea to look at what this term entails. The core textbook *Working with Texts* provides a useful metaphor arising out of the **etymology** (the source and development) of the word:

> The word **text** itself originally meant 'something woven' (Latin *texere, textum* - 'to weave'), and you can see a relationship between text, textile ('capable of being woven') and texture ('having the quality of woven cloth'). Written language is also often referred to as 'material'.
>
> (Carter et al. 1997: 166)

If we think of texts as woven material, then we could say that the fabric of magazines resembles a patchwork quilt. We will examine the ways in which magazine text producers manipulate different aspects of language to give their material texture.

Tracing patterns in language

The following activity involves reassembling two features from two different magazines. One is from *Cosmopolitan*, 'Get Eurosavvy!', and the other is from *FHM Bionic*, 'The icy plunge'. Sentences taken randomly have been mixed together. Try to reconstruct the two features; then check by looking at the originals on pp. 89–90. The features are not complete, only the first two paragraphs are used. Here's the first sentence of each to get you started: 'Europe's cool' and 'Canyoning is a summer sport'.

Activity

1   After all, jumping off a cliff into churning icy water is behaviour suitable only for the insane – so I've decided that I may as well go the whole hog.
2   Europe's cool.
3   Canyoning is a summer sport. Therefore, obviously, I've chosen a severe blizzard in mid-November to give it a go.
4   British music no longer has the monopoly on cool and who says French or Italian designers are best?
5   We demand adventure, excitement and allure.
6   We want interesting sounds, exotic tastes and sexy freedom – and we want it this weekend please!
7   But amazingly, at the Cascade d'Angon, above the village of Talloires and Lake Annecy in southern France, there is no shortage of fear junkies and thrill-seekers eager to take the plunge themselves.
8   Boundaries are breaking down, so are old rules.
9   Sixty metres sheer drop down a smooth limestone chute, an icy stream pours down from the French Alps.
10   Modern women ignore the sceptics and reap the benefits of the Continent; we're looking outside ourselves and our country for our kicks.
11   A rickety guard-rail is all that keeps you from plummeting into unseen depths.
12   We're as likely to go to a hen party in Barcelona as in the local Spanish restaurant, as happy about being seconded to the company's Milan office as its Manchester subsidiary.
13   The chute is hidden deep in a canyon whose only access is via a narrow path notched into the limestone cliff-face.
14   There's never been a better time to immerse yourself in the thrill of being part of the most exciting continent on earth – the home of couture, culture and cappuccino.

83

15   And the deluge carries on for another 30m before tearing into the pool below.
16   As the path reaches the waterfall – at roughly halfway – a hissing plume roars straight out of a hole in the sky some 30ft above.
17   There are glorious opportunities to be had, and they're all just a train ride away.
18   What are you waiting for?
19   Not only are we ready to embrace Europe, we can imagine ourselves *living* there.
20   Nearing the rickety fence for a peek over the edge turns my usually hearty stomach to a pit of nausea. And I feel only a calm regret as I mutter a vague, desperate plea to the Lord and stumble towards it trying not to think about the jump I'm facing.

You will probably find that you were able to separate the texts quite easily and to reconstruct them without too many mistakes. The reason you were able to do this is because each text has distinct patterns running through it that help the reader to make sense of it. One of the strategies you used was your understanding of words and phrases in the English language. In particular, your awareness of the relationships between words. This is referred to as lexical cohesion.

Lexical cohesion

Lexical cohesion refers to the way aspects of vocabulary link parts of texts together. Some of the lexical patterns are:

◎ Direct repetition (exactly the same word repeated)

> *Cosmopolitan* We want . . . we want
> *FHM Bionic* chute . . . chute

◎   Synonyms (words with very similar meanings)

> *Cosmopolitan* demand . . . want
> *FHM Bionic* jump . . . plunge

◎ Superordination (where one word encompasses another in meaning)

Cosmopolitan Europe's ... British, French, Italian

◎   Antonyms (opposites)

        FHM Bionic above ... below

◎   Specific to general reference (where the same thing or person is referred to, but the first reference has more detail)

        Cosmopolitan interesting sounds, exotic tastes and sexy freedom ... it

◎   Ordered series (words that we know as a set of series, e.g. the days of the week, months of the year, etc.)

        FHM Bionic sixty metres ... 30ft ... 30m

A much more general aspect of lexical cohesion is the use by writers of particular semantic fields. This means referring to a specific area of experience or knowledge. In the feature from *FHM Bionic* 'The icy plunge', the semantic field is canyoning: 'cliff-face', 'chute', 'canyon'.

     The patterns of word choice in the texts are centred around adventure and thrills. Similar words are used to describe two entirely different types of experience. The *Cosmopolitan* text is about 'knowing where to shop, what to say, how to party and where to play'. The *FHM Bionic* text is about a different type of activity, canyoning; a sport for 'adrenalin junkies' that seems to exclude women since only men are featured in the text.

Grammatical cohesion

Your understanding of grammatical structures is another strategy which helped you to reassemble the texts. The way that grammatical features are woven across sentence boundaries is referred to as grammatical cohesion. Some of the grammatical patterns are:

◎   Reference
        This tells the reader that they can only make complete sense of the word or structure they are looking at if they look elsewhere in the text to get a fuller picture. Particular words are used for reference purposes:

◎　Personal pronouns

These are words that can substitute for nouns, e.g. 'I', 'you', 'he', 'she', and 'it'. In Text: 'The icy plunge', 'there' acts as a pronoun which refers to something coming later (this is referred to as cataphoric reference):

> ... **there** is no shortage of fear junkies and thrill seekers eager to take the plunge themselves.

When the pronoun refers back to something, this is called anaphoric reference:

> Canyoning is a summer sport. Therefore obviously I've chosen a severe blizzard in mid-November to give **it** a go.

'It' refers back to canyoning. Imagine how repetitive texts would be if we didn't have such terms:

> Canyoning is a summer sport. Therefore obviously I've chosen a severe blizzard in mid-November to give canyoning a go.

Sometimes the reader has to look for information outside of the text, this is referred to as exophoric reference. An example of this is when the pronoun 'you' occurs in a text, the reader knows they are to insert themselves as the reference point. Text: 'Get Eurosavvy!' uses the reflexive pronoun:

> Europe's cool. There's never been a better time to immerse **yourself** in the thrill of being part of the most exciting continent on earth – the home of couture, culture and cappuccino.

When the text is completely self-contained, i.e. not needing any support from outside, this is referred to as endophoric reference. This is so rare in magazines it was difficult to find an example.

◎　Demonstrative reference (deictics)

Another type of reference is signalled by words such as 'the', 'this', 'that', 'these', 'those', 'here', and 'there'. These are referred to as verbal pointers because they tell the reader where something is, as in the example from Text: 'Get Eurosavvy!'

> Not only are we ready to embrace Europe, we can imagine our-
> selves *living* **there**.

Look through the two texts for some more examples of words
which point something out.

◎ Comparative reference

Comparative reference tells the reader not just to look elsewhere in
the text but to look with a specific purpose in mind.

> There's never been a **better** time to immerse yourself in the
> thrill of being part of the **most** exciting continent on earth –
> the home of couture, culture and cappuccino.

Comparatives are the second term in a three term system of
comparison, e.g. good/better/best. Superlatives are the third term,
e.g. exciting/more exciting/most exciting. In these examples the
reference point is omitted. What is the effect of this?

◎ Substitution and ellipsis

Substitution, as it suggests, means that the writer has substituted
one item for another, for example 'deluge' stands in for 'a hissing
plume'.

> – a hissing plume roars straight out of a hole in the sky some
> 30ft above. And the deluge carries on for another 30m before
> tearing into the pool below.

◎ Ellipsis

Surprisingly, missing something out can actually cause texts to
cohere.

> After all, jumping off a cliff into churning icy water is
> behaviour suitable only for the insane – so I've decided that
> I may as well go the whole hog.

In the interests of economy of expression the text producer has not
added 'and jump off a cliff into churning icy water'. Meaning is
not obscured since the reader can easily fill in the gaps.

◎   Conjunctions

Perhaps the best known form of joining parts of texts together are through the words used specially for this purpose, known as **conjunctions**. There are two types of conjunctions: **co-ordinating** conjunctions, e.g. 'and', 'but' and 'so':

> Boundaries are breaking down, **so** are old rules

and **subordinating** conjunctions which join subordinate clauses to a main clause, e.g. 'after', 'although', 'until' 'when', 'whether', etc. Look at the various uses of 'as' in the following example:

> We're as likely to go to a hen night in Barcelona as in the local Spanish restaurant, as happy about being seconded to the company's Milan office as its Manchester subsidiary.

Get Eurosavvy!

136 ways to get on top in Europe

Doing the Continental means knowing where to shop, what to say, how to party and where to play.

Europe's cool. There's never been a better time to immerse yourself in the thrill of being part of the most exciting continent on earth – the home of couture, culture and cappuccino.

Boundaries are breaking down, so are old rules. British music no longer has the monopoly on cool and who says French or Italian designers are best? Modern women ignore the sceptics and reap the benefits of the Continent; we're looking outside ourselves and our country for our kicks. We demand adventure, excitement and allure. We want interesting sounds, exotic tastes and sexy freedom – and we want it this weekend please!

Not only are we ready to embrace Europe, we can imagine ourselves *living* there. We're as likely to go to a hen night in Barcelona as in the local Spanish restaurant, as happy about being seconded to the company's Milan office as its Manchester subsidiary. There are glorious opportunities to be had, and they're all just a train ride away. What are you waiting for? >

12 FABULOUS EUROPHILES to know now – at least by sight

Björk · Alexander McQueen · Damon Albarn · John Galliano · Air · Stella McCartney · Daft Punk · Kristin Scott Thomas · Joaquín Cortés · George Michael · Gianluca Vialli · Elton John

The icy plunge

The sport of canyoning is heaven-sent for adrenalin junkies seeking a weekend top-up. *FHM Bionic* joins the crevasse-leapers in France

WORDS: RORY O'CALLAGHAN PHOTOGRAPHY: NICKY WOOD

The Cascade d'Angon in Southern France: home to thrill-seekers

CANYONING IS A summer sport. Therefore, obviously, I've chosen a severe blizzard in mid-November to give it a go. After all, jumping off a cliff into churning icy water is behaviour suitable only for the insane – so I've decided that I may as well go the whole hog. But amazingly, at the Cascade d'Angon, above the village of Talloires and Lake Annecy in southern France, there is no shortage of fear junkies and thrill-seekers eager to take the plunge themselves. Sixty metres sheer drop down a smooth limestone chute, an icy stream pours down from the French Alps.

The chute is hidden deep in a canyon whose only access is via a narrow path notched into the limestone cliff-face. A rickety guard-rail is all that keeps you from plummeting into unseen depths. As the path reaches the waterfall – at roughly halfway – a hissing plume roars straight out of a hole in the sky some 30ft above. And the deluge carries on for another 30m before tearing into the pool below. Nearing the rickety fence for a peek over the edge turns my usually hearty stomach to a pit of nausea. And I feel only a calm regret as I mutter a vague, desperate plea to the Lord and stumble towards it trying not to think about the jump I'm facing.

A single wetsuit should have been enough to absorb the impact, but with our pool almost frozen solid, three are necessary. Fantasies of resembling 007 swiftly disappear as Regis – the group leader – advises simply pissing ourselves to avoid the trouble of suit removal.

As the instruction sinks in, we watch him hook up to a bolt set into the limestone. These are about 15cm deep and will expand if they start to slip out – which makes them fantastically secure, apparently. Standing on a 10cm ledge, Regis, staring straight into the abyss, still looks like he's waiting for a number 16 bus.

His assistant Eric follows, attaching a long rope to another bolt and throwing it into the cascade. Moments later he has attached the rope to his harness and disappeared into the foam.

Opening my eyes again, I see Regis motioning to hook up. That's the easy bit. Immediately I'm quivering, and pointing at the guard-rail, as if to say, "You want me to climb over this? To the far side?" He simply nods. So I tentatively clamber over and look down.

"No!" That was my only thought. "No, I'm not really doing this. I'm not standing on top of ▷

Three wetsuits halt my Bond fantasy

Canyoning is a mixture of swimming, abseiling and rock scrambling

90

Look back at any of the texts you have worked with and try to find examples of lexical and grammatical cohesion.

The discourse of magazines

The next section will examine larger patterns relating to the social dimensions of the text, e.g. the ideological implications of the language choices made. Text: 'The Importance of Being a Posh Footballer', referred to in unit three, pp. 26–7 is a parody of a working-class newspaper. The story was commissioned, supposedly, to discover whether a 'posh footballer' was a possibility, but it seems to be more of an opportunity to lampoon working-class people.

You might attempt an analysis of Text: 'The importance of being a posh footballer.' Try to implement the suggestions made throughout the book. To get a sense of the ideological stance taken by the text producer, look in particular at points in the text where reference is made to class divisions in society. Also, are there any points where the magazine format is still present?

The layout is that of a tabloid newspaper associated with working-class people. The images accompanying the written text are boxed in, which is typical of the newspaper format. The text is written in regular columns. There is no use of colour or variety in the font styles used. However, unlike most newspapers, the pictures are in colour. The title has been made to look like the *Sun*'s.

Some of the poetic features referred to in unit two are present:

◎ Rhyme – Ginola says '"Ooh la la" as football goes la-di-da.' Here the text producer mimics the speech of middle-class people.
◎ Pun – 'French polish' is a play on words since this can be a treatment for good quality wooden furniture, again a class association. In the context of the feature it is referring to Ginola's nationality and football skill.

◎   Alliteration – 'pukka players'
◎   Intertextuality – 'The importance of being a posh footballer' is a reference to Oscar Wilde's play, *The Importance of Being Earnest*.

Patterns of word choices

It's hardly likely that upper/middle-class people refer to themselves as 'posh', rather this is what they are known as in working-class circles. 'Pukka' is a word associated with the upper/middle classes. It came into the English language in the seventeenth century from Hindi, 'pakka', meaning 'firm'. In English it means 'genuine' or 'good'. 'Gin Fizz' is a drink associated with the upper/middle classes.

The magazine format is still present with the details of products supplied:

> David Ginola wears Hawk overhead cagoule with reflective logo and taping, £75; colour block cargo pants, £45, both by Admiral. For details, see Stockists.

The subject position which the text producer constructs for the reader is someone who is familiar with the institutions mentioned: 'Westminster', 'Eton' and 'Gordonstoun'. In fact, these places are so familiar they have become speaking subjects i.e. human qualities have been attributed to an inanimate form, a process known as **personification**:

> Gordonstoun **describes** football as its 'weakness'. . . .
> Bryanston **admits** to having 'no fixtures'. . . .
> Rugby **confirms** that it's not called that for nothing.

The text producer also appeals to the reader's sense of nationalism by using the possessive pronoun:

> Football is **our** national game and footballers are **our** national heroes.

This close relationship is continued in references to other areas of social life which are thought to be shared by the reader:

> They date **our** pop stars and TV personalities. . . .
> In short, with their strong legs and seven-figure salaries, footballers are **our** new aristocracy.

The text reveals the snobbery of *Tatler* in labouring the point that footballers are usually from working-class origins. The examples cited are stereotypical and rely on the reader's existing knowledge:

> Take, for example, the lager-fuelled antics of the pre-Priory Gazza. Or the black-eyed pictures of Ulrika Jonnson and Sheryl Gascoigne taken after arguments with their respective footballer partners.

'The gin fizz-fuelled antics' would not have quite the same ring. Although the feature is meant to be written from the viewpoint of the working class, albeit a parody, this group is not represented in a favourable light.

Extension

As you have seen, parodies are useful exercises since they do not attempt a faithful replication of the original, instead they present a caricature of the genre. You might like to try imitating the magazine format by writing an article on a topic of your choice. By exaggerating the form, this should highlight the structure of the text so far as its grammar, style and word choice are concerned.

Summary

This unit has attempted to illustrate the linguistic devices which cause texts to hang together by examining lexical and grammatical cohesion. It has also explored the concept 'discourse' and shown ways which language can convey the ideological stance of the text's producer by their appeals to shared values and careful lexical choices.

93

Representations of women and men
Constructing femininity, masculinity and sexuality

The aim of this unit is to examine the processes whereby femininity, masculinity and sexuality are constructed through the language of magazines. The unit will take into account the changes currently taking place in society, for example, to reflect the impact that feminism has made and also that men are beginning to be addressed in ways which previously only women were. The unit will also explore the communities which readers are invited to join based on their consumption of commodities.

Unit two introduced the idea that magazines are a means of presenting ideal-reader images to which the purchaser can aspire. The notion that our social identities are constructed through language was introduced in unit five and some of the linguistic tools used were illustrated. We will attempt to relate these two concepts, but before doing so it must be noted that on reading a magazine, readers are already constituted in other discourses such as education, the example given in unit six. Although society has some very clear views about what constitutes appropriate femininity, masculinity and sexuality, these are by no means stable or unitary, so it might be more appropriate to refer to these in the plural – femininities, masculinities and sexualities.

Femininities and masculinities

What is understood by these terms? In unit four, on examining horoscopes, we saw a number of perspectives on what was considered to be appropriate feminine behaviour, for example, putting one's own feelings to one side and caring about others. This can be contrasted with the editor's letter from the male magazine we looked at, which presented a view of masculinity as aggressive behaviour, although it did so in a self-mocking, ironic way. Talbot (1998) suggests that we might turn 'feminine' into a verb, 'to feminise'.

> Femininity is articulated in and through commercial and mass media discourses, especially in the magazine industry and in the fashion industries of clothing and cosmetics. But most of all, it is articulated on women's bodies, by women themselves.
>
> (1998: 171)

By turning *femininity* into a verb it highlights the active process whereby women readily engage in the various practices which are needed to make them appear appropriately feminine. A further point to make is that femininity is culturally specific. An example to illustrate this would be the recent media hype when the actor Julia Roberts was reported to have been spotted with visible underarm hair. Underarm hair on women in the West is considered by many to be unfeminine, yet in other cultures not to remove underarm hair is considered to be as normal as hair growth itself. Femininity is also historically specific. To illustrate this we could compare magazines from two different eras.

Activity

Text: 'Knit a Jumper for your Dog' is taken from a 1935 edition of *The Girl's Own Paper* and Text: 'Snog Guide' is from a 1997 edition of *J-17*. Both texts are instructional and are aimed at young women.

What differences are there in relation to constructions of femininity?

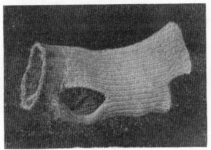

The finished jumper

Knit a Jumper for Your Dog

MANY girls can knit such nice woolly jumpers for dolls, and it is just as easy to make them for small dogs who will be so grateful when the icy winds blow.

Of course, some small dogs have thick hairy coats of their own and don't need anything more, but there are several little fellows with very thin ones who feel the cold very much, and to buy them proper cloth coats cost quite a lot of money. Then there is always the chance that one day *Little Fido* will take it into his head to have a good roll in the mud and his beautiful cloth coat with its smart braid will be a sad sight. But if he wears a woolly jumper you can just tell him what you think of his naughty ways, pop the jumper in the wash tub, and out it comes as good as new.

Even if you have never done much knitting, you have only to follow these directions carefully and you will find it is not difficult to make a dog's jumper.

SUPPOSING you want one for a dog about the size of a Cairn Terrier, you will need 2 oz. of 4-ply fingering. A dark brown colour or a dark mixture looks nice. Don't ask him to go out in pale pink or sky blue—you never know what dogs say to each other— and don't make woolly boots to match, for he won't be a bit grateful, believe me !

You will want four No. 9 needles and four No. 7.

Cast on 72 stitches on No. 9 needles and knit 2 plain 2 purl for 2½ inches. Then divide the stitches in half and put them on No. 7 needles.

On the one half, working on two No. 7 needles knit 5 inches in stocking stitch ; on the other half, working on No. 7 needles knit 5 inches of knit 1 purl 1.

Now join up and work again on four needles (No. 7) knit 1 purl 1 for about 8 inches. This depends on the length of the dog's back and you must measure him. Let the jumper cover his ribs, but do not let it get in his way underneath and make him uncomfortable. A little lady dog can have more length left under her tummy.

When you have knitted the right length, cast off 36 stitches on the half of the jumper that has the stocking stitch ; this is the under part of the jumper.

On the other half of the jumper continue the knitting on two needles, knit 1 purl 1 for 4 inches, and then cast off.

JANE BEVAN.

Don't make woolly boots to match, for he won't be a bit grateful !

97

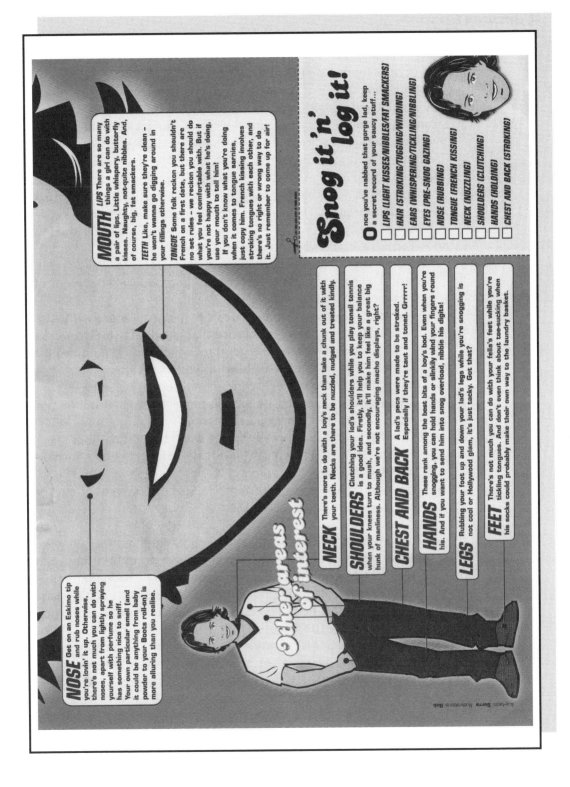

NOSE Get on an Eskimo tip and rub noses while you're lovin' it up. Otherwise, there's not much you can do with noses, apart from lightly spraying yourself with perfume so he has something nice to sniff. Your own particular smell (and it could be anything from baby powder to your Boots roll-on) is more alluring than you realise.

MOUTH *LIPS* There are so many things a girl can do with a pair of lips. Little whispery, butterfly kisses. Naughty, not-quite nibbles. And, of course, big, fat smackers.

TEETH Like, make sure they're clean – he won't wanna go digging around in your fillings otherwise.

TONGUE Some folk reckon you shouldn't French on a first date, but there are no set rules – we reckon you should do what you feel comfortable with. But if you're not happy with what he's doing, use your mouth to tell him! If you don't know what you're doing when it comes to tongue sarnies, just copy him. French kissing involves stroking tongues with each other, and there's no right or wrong way to do it. Just remember to come up for air!

Other areas of interest

NECK There's more to do with a boy's neck than take a chunk out of it with your teeth. Necks are there to be nuzzled, nudged and treated kindly.

SHOULDERS Clutching your lad's shoulders while you play tonsil tennis is a good idea. Firstly, it'll help you to keep your balance when your knees turn to mush, and secondly, it'll make him feel like a great big hunk of manliness. Although we're not encouraging macho displays, right?

CHEST AND BACK A lad's pecs were made to be stroked. Especially if they're taut and toned. Grrrrr!

HANDS These rank among the best bits of a boy's bod. Even when you're snogging, you can hold hands or slinkily wind your fingers round his. And if you want to send him into snog overload, nibble his digits!

LEGS Rubbing your foot up and down your lad's legs while you're snogging is not cool or Hollywood glam, it's just tacky. Got that?

FEET There's not much you can do with your fella's feet while you're tickling tongues. And don't even think about toe-sucking when his socks could probably make their own way to the laundry basket.

Snog it 'n' log it!

Once you've nabbed that gorge lad, keep a secret record of your saucy stuff...

- [ ] LIPS (LIGHT KISSES/NIBBLES/FAT SMACKERS)
- [ ] HAIR (STROKING/TUGGING/WINDING)
- [ ] EARS (WHISPERING/TICKLING/NIBBLING)
- [ ] EYES (PRE-SNOG GAZING)
- [ ] NOSE (RUBBING)
- [ ] TONGUE (FRENCH KISSING)
- [ ] NECK (NUZZLING)
- [ ] SHOULDERS (CLUTCHING)
- [ ] HANDS (HOLDING)
- [ ] CHEST AND BACK (STROKING)

Commentary

Text: 'Knit a Jumper for your Dog', believe it or not, is indeed a set of instructions for making the said garment. Although the tone is similar to that found in modern magazines, the voice of a friendly expert, modern readers would no doubt think the text is a joke. This is largely due to the absurdity of the activity, but also due to the language used by the text producer, which seems to fit the stereotypical patterns of 'women's language' as proposed by Lakoff (1975). According to Lakoff, women use more of certain features which makes their language lack forcefulness. It is important to note that her observations have not been substantiated by empirical research. The features present in the text are:

- Forms which convey impreciseness, e.g. 'such':
  Many girls can knit **such** nice woolly jumpers for dolls, and it is just as easy to make them for small dogs who will be so grateful when the icy winds blow.
- Forms which express emotional rather than intellectual evaluation:
  Then there is always the chance that one day Little Fido will take it into his head to have a good roll in the mud and his beautiful cloth coat with its smart braid will be a sad sight.
- Intensifiers: for example, 'so' in 'so grateful'.
- Diminutives (to convey the meaning small or to express affection): e.g. 'several little fellows'.
- Qualifiers: for example, 'a bit' in 'he won't be a bit grateful'.
- Politeness: for example, 'a little lady dog' (a polite way of avoiding 'bitch'), also 'under her tummy' (avoids stomach).
- Hedging: for example, 'supposing' in 'Supposing you want one for a dog about the size of a Cairn Terrier.'

The text producer's expectations of the readers are that they are young women with lots of time on their hands and not much in the way of entertainment. Not only does the text convey a very patronising attitude towards the reader, incredibly, it has homophobic undertones in relation to the dog: 'Don't ask him to go out in pale pink or sky blue – you never know what dogs say to each other –.' No doubt some people do talk to animals but usually this is spontaneous, they're not told what to say.

Text: 'Snog Guide' is a set of instructions for a different kind of activity, 'snogging'. On scanning modern magazines aimed at young women, there is an absence of craftwork to enable a true comparison to be made. This is hardly surprising given that the motivation of modern magazines is to encourage the consumption of ready-made commodities.

You will see that the language of the text producer is quite different. Although the tone is still friendly, the relationship seems to be more on a level with the reader. The text producer attempts to use the language of the reader which is quite informal: for example, 'bonce' instead of 'head', 'peepers' instead of 'eyes'. There are colloquial expressions, 'get to grips'. There are examples of informal grammar – 'kinda' instead of 'kind of' and 'wanna' instead of 'want to'. There are also some traces of so-called 'women's features' – the expressive form 'Little whispery, butterfly kisses' – and imprecise forms – 'Naughty, **not-quite** nibbles'. However, these are countered by the behaviour being advocated which is still fairly rebellious, even by today's standards. Before we get complacent, however, young women are still being told what to do and we must also question whose interests are being served by young women improving their 'snogging' technique.

Of course, all of the above points in relation to femininity can be said of masculinity. Men too are constantly being invoked to work towards achieving and maintaining their masculinities.

It is well documented that the contents of magazines are not randomly selected and that market researchers have sophisticated methods of studying consumers. They pass this information on to editors who can then provide what the public have been shown to desire. This is a complex process, however, since it is never clear which came first, the desire or the compulsion to desire.

As already stated, magazines are underpinned by advertising revenue, which can easily be illustrated by how much space is given to advertisements. As a consequence, advertisers have an influential role in deciding the content of magazines. It was pointed out in unit two that a current trend in magazines aimed at women and men, both teenage and adult markets, is the intensification of interest in the topic of sex. Being attractive to the opposite sex, it is suggested, involves a certain amount of labour and the consumption of numerous goods which readers are encouraged to purchase through advertising and various features. The question of the magazine's content and the consumption of goods are therefore intricately linked.

Constructing femininities and masculinities: the advertorial

Advertorials are features which are specially written to encourage consumption of the products mentioned in them.

PULSE

FACIAL HYGIENE
Scrub it!

Sploshing your face every morning with warm water and a bit of gungy soap is only going to give you blackheads and a nasty rash. Here's how to take proper care of your boat

Leonard easily took Gold in the freelance spitting section

4 Paste your blackheads...
The black dot you see isn't dirt – the oily plug turns black when it's exposed to air. Use a concentrated paste to help unclog pores, draw out blackheads and prevent further problems. Try Kiehls Repairateur Drawing Paste, £12.50 for 14g, or Body Shop Japanese Washing Grains, £2.05 for 50g. Apply only to the spotty area and rinse off.

5 ...or squeeze the bastards
If a blackhead looks ready to go, you can gently extract it. Wrap your fingertips in tissue (to avoid spreading bacteria) and press together to oust the blemish. Do not gouge it out with your fingernails. Clumsy squeezing makes the contents of the blackhead spread into surrounding tissue, causing inflammation and leaving you worse off than before.

1 Use a cleanser
Wash your face every day using a rinse-off cleanser, not soap or shower gel. This will be specially pH balanced to match your skin type and so won't aggravate it. Oily or spotty skin: Elemis Spot Control Wash, £7.95 for 125ml. Dry skin: Aveda Gel Cleanser, £7 for 53ml. Normal skin: Body Shop Mostly Men Face Wash, £3.95 for 100ml.

6 Dare to use a face mask
It'll deep-clean, moisturise, and soften the skin. Do it in the bath because (a) no one will see you, and (b) the steam will help the mask to work better. Oily or spotty skin: Kiehls Rare Earth Face Masque, £13.50 for 118ml. Dry skin: Espa Essential Mineral Mask, £14.95 for 60g. Normal skin: Body Shop Peanut and Rosehip Mask, £4.15 for 100ml.

2 Wipe with lotion
Go over your face with a cotton ball soaked in astringent lotion. This gets rid of any traces of the cleanser, and gives skin that bracing 'cold shower' feel. Oily or spotty skin: Aramis Skin Clearing Solution, £12 for 100ml. Dry skin: Kiehls Cucumber Herbal Toner, £7.95 for 118ml. Normal skin: Espa Herbal Spafresh, £9.95 for 100ml.

7 Finish with moisturiser
Use it daily to keep skin smooth and protect against the elements. Choose one with sun filters, even in winter. You might have noticed products containing AHA (alpha hydroxy acid), a much-hyped ingredient. It is derived from fruit, and helps dissolve dead skin cells, dirt and oil, leaving skin fresher and clearer. Find it in the new Polo Sport skincare range, as well as Aramis and Clinique products.
Oily or spotty skin: Vichy Basic Homme Total Day Care, £10 for 50ml. Dry skin: Espa Essential Protective Serum, £18.50 for 30ml. Normal skin: Polo Sport Face Fitness AHA Moisture Formula, £15 for 75ml. **(LB)**

3 Scrub off dead skin
Facial scrub is a gel containing tiny granules which lift off dirt and dead skin cells. Lightly massage a small dollop into your skin, avoiding the eyes and concentrating on the nose and chin. If you suffer from flaky lips, gently rub it into them too. Rinse off with water. Try Polo Sport Fragrance Free Scrub Face Wash, £11 – it cleanses too.

SKINCARE STOCKISTS

Aramis: All leading chemists and department stores
Aveda: Call 0171-636 7911
Body Shop: Stores nationwide
Elemis: Call 0181-954 8033

Espa: Call 01483 454444
Kiehls: Call 0171-379 7030
Polo Sport: House of Fraser, Boots
Tweezerman: Call 171-636 7911
Vichy: Boots, Harrods and Selfridges

PHOTOGRAPHY: ADRIAN COOK; STYLING: ISSY VIRDEN; HAIR AND MAKE-UP: LINDA BURNS; MODEL: SHANE AT NEVS

catwalk beauty

Brand nude
Dare to go bare with the new take on all that's natural.

As seen at Cerruti, Jil Sander, Byblos, Todd Oldham, Louis Vuitton, Marc Jacobs

Essential for Laid back confidence. Great if you have little time to spare and even less inclination to spend hours in front of the mirror.

Why it works "There is always a demand for a natural look, as some women will never want to wear a lot of make-up. But the relevance is wider now because it suits the current mood of minimalism," says Linda Cantello, make-up artist at Jil Sander. "There's something intimidating and off-putting about a woman who is overly made-up. To me, it says insecurity and looks dated."

How to pull it off

This season, natural really means natural. "It's not so artificial any more," says Linda Cantello. "Yet we can still get away with a few tricks without anybody realising we've done anything at all.

"To make it slightly different this season, I decided on a glossy eye. I mixed a golden brown cream with Elizabeth Arden Eight-Hour Cream and smeared it across the lid. It was very subtle and only noticeable as the models blinked. There was minimal concealer to hide the blemishes and a lip mattifier to take the colour out of the mouth," adds Cantello. If you do little else, pay attention to the brows and lashes – two key elements of the season. A layer of mascara and a brush of brow colour will frame and lift the face. >

What to use (clockwise from top left):

Origins Just Browsing, £9

Estée Lauder Minimalist Mascara, £13.50

Kiehl's Ultra Moisturising Concealer Stick, £19.50

Lancôme Lip Brio in Transparent Sharon, £11.50

Activity

Compare texts: Pulse from *FHM* with Brand nude from *Cosmopolitan*. How is masculinity constructed in 'Pulse'? How is femininity constructed in 'Brand nude'? You might find the checklist supplied in unit five helpful.

Commentary

Text: Pulse

Layout

There is a mixture of written text and visual images. The largest image is in the top left-hand corner and shows an upper body shot of a male who has been soaked with water. The written text which anchors the image says: 'Leonard easily took Gold in the freelance spitting section.' This turns the activity of cleansing into a sport. Smaller images accompany the step-by-step instructions, each of which advertise a beauty product to be used in the routine. The header is a command 'Scrub it!' and the subtext refers to the imagined current washing habits of the reader: 'Sploshing your face every morning with warm water and a bit of gungy soap is only going to give you blackheads and a nasty rash. Here's how to take proper care of your boat.'

The identity of the text producer

There are no pronouns to give a clue as to whether the text is singly or multiply authored. The writer appears to be an expert on cleansing, but attempts to make the feature friendly by using language with which the reader will be familiar. There is an attempt to entertain: 'boat race' is Cockney rhyming slang for face. The writer appears certain in her assertions: 'This **will** be specially pH balanced to match your skin type and so won't aggravate it.' She is less certain in making assumptions about the reader's knowledge of products available: 'You **might** have noticed products containing AHA (alpha hydroxy acid), a much hyped ingredient.' Presumably, if the reader already knows about such products, they wouldn't need the expert advice of the text producer.

The identity of the reader

The text producer addresses the reader directly by using the pronouns 'you' and 'your' as though the reader is known to her. There is a presupposition that the reader's current practice is to 'splosh' their face, whatever this might mean. It is also assumed that they would not like to be caught in the act of cleansing: 'Do it in the bath because (a) no one will see you, and (b) the steam will help the mask to work better.' The text producer also puts the reader in the picture on a presumed misapprehension: 'The black dot you see isn't dirt — the oily plug turns black when it's exposed to air.' It is as though the reader has said 'the black dot is dirt'.

Text: Brand nude

Layout

Again there is a mixture of written text and visual images. A large photograph of a model's face appears in the top right-hand corner of the page. There are four similar images which are smaller and one of a model, presumably on a catwalk because she looks as though she is walking. This is not boxed but has the text wrapped around it. The header 'Brand nude' is a pun on the phrase 'brand new'. 'Nude', in the context of the article, refers to a practice in makeup which is for the wearer not to look as though she is wearing makeup. The reader is caused to think about 'new' as in the latest trend in fashion. The subtext, 'Dare to go bare with the new take on all that's natural', dares the reader to go without makeup. There are three subheadings: 'Essential for', 'Why it works', which presupposes that the reader is going to be asking these questions, and the third one, 'How to pull it off', presupposes she will ultimately want to have a go. Some of the written text is colour co-ordinated to complement the 'natural look'.

The identity of the text producer

The writer is someone who has insider knowledge of what is happening behind the scenes of the catwalk. She has access to others who are 'in the know' and quotes their views '"There's always a demand for a natural look . . ." says Linda Cantello, make-up artist at Jil Sander.' The reader is presumed to know that Jil Sander is a leading fashion designer. The writer is assertive in what she says: 'This season, natural really means natural.'

105

The identity of the reader

Again the reader is personally addressed. Since she is 'dare(d) to go bare' it is presumed that women are reluctant to go without makeup, yet the number of products needed to achieve this 'look' is incredible. Statements such as 'This season, natural really means natural' acknowledges a taken for granted assumption that looks change from season to season. It also suggests that the utterance has been said before to the reader but half-heartedly. The reference to the natural look being essential for 'Laid back confidence' creates a link between how women look on the outside and what they feel on the inside.

Comparison of the texts

Both texts have in common an attempt to promote the products mentioned in that brand names and prices are included. In the men's feature the stockists are also included, which suggests that men are thought to be unfamiliar with where to buy beauty products. Whereas men are urged to start a beauty regime, it is taken as axiomatic that women will already be engaged in such activities. Men are addressed as though they are likely to feel less masculine by engaging in beauty work. It is ironic that women are also being encouraged to do something but this time the attempt is to get them looking as though they are not engaging in beauty work. A double irony is that to achieve the 'natural look' they are being sold the same amount of products. The vocabulary choices are interesting in that men are told to 'scrub', a word which conveys an abrasive action, whereas women are told to 'smear': 'I mixed a golden brown cream with Elizabeth Arden Eight-Hour Cream and smeared it across the lid.'

The material contained in the next few pages may prove too explicit for some readers since it presents the coverage in magazines of the topic of sex. You may want to skip this section but it should not adversely affect your reading of the rest of the book. Throughout this textbook there have been references to the apparent preoccupation of contemporary magazine text producers with the topic of sex. This seems to be the case whether the target audience is female, male, teenage or adult. It was felt that to write a book on the language of magazines without discussing a major concern would make it incomplete. The illicitness of the material on offer in magazines is usually heavily foregrounded by emblazoning it on the front cover, e.g. 'The 5 second sex **secret**' (*Cosmopolitan*). The next section will consider whether the text producers' claims concerning the transgressive nature of the material has any merit.

Constructing sexuality

Position of the fortnight is a regular feature in *More!* which purports to inform readers of sex techniques. Although it is not directly linked to the sale of goods advertised in the magazine, in encouraging readers to become sexually active it supports an ideology which espouses that to become sexually attractive involves the purchase and consumption of beauty products.

It can prove interesting to examine the language which text producers choose when describing relationships or actions between women and men. In particular you could focus on the relationship between the verb (or verb group), the participants in the action, state or process and other elements of the clause. This is referred to as **transitivity**. Halliday (1985) devised a model for analysing transitivity. Transitivity is concerned with the clause which is made up of three parts:

1   The *process*, whether material, mental, or relational. Material processes involve verbs such as 'walk', mental processes involve verbs such as 'think' and relational processes relate items, e.g. 'He **is** arrogant.'
2   The *participants* in the process.
3   The *circumstances* of the process.

Activity

Who is given the prominent role in the Text: 'Position of the fortnight?' To help answer this, look at the material processes, these involve 'doing'. There are two possible roles, the Agent who 'does' the action and the Goal who is affected by the action:

The cat (Agent) chased (process) the dog (Goal)

The Agent is always present in the process but the Goal is optional:

The cat (Agent) meows (process) (no goal).

In clauses where both Agent and Goal are present, the Agent can be emphasised by the choice of active voice or the Goal may be the focus by becoming the grammatical subject and choosing the passive voice.

The cat chased the dog (active voice)
The dog was chased by the cat (passive voice)

Note that there is the option of deleting the Agent: The dog was chased.

107

Text: Position of the fortnight

The roll-over
Bust those post-hols blues with this sensuous, easy move.

Getting it right
Lie on your front with your legs apart. Keep your head and shoulders raised while leaning on your elbows. He lies between your legs and enters you, grasping you with one arm and gently rolling back so that you are both lying on your sides – still connected. Once you're steady, lean a little on to your back and raise your bum so he can thrust without slipping out. Meanwhile, he can hold his weight up by putting his hand in front of your body and pushing up.

What's in it for you
Total body contact and penetration and a feeling of luxurious comfort.

Special requirements
A relaxed mind and body.
        (*More!* 15–28 January 1997)

Text: Mind the leather

3 STAIRS
Best position: She kneels on the second step from the top of the landing. bottom in the air, body bent forward, head resting on her hands and legs as far apart as stairs permit.
Technique: Enter your beloved from behind.
Advantages: This position permits all-round support and lots of handholds (other stairs, banisters) for grip and extra thrust.
Sensible precautions: Make sure you've got a firm grip – how are you going to explain lying naked at the bottom of the stairs to the ambulance crew? Friction or carpet burns can be painful (though providing trophies). It's semi-public so make sure visiting grannies are not prowling after midnight.
        (*Men's Health* July/August 1998)

Commentary

In Text: 'Position of the fortnight', the reader must insert themselves into the text, as the Agent of several proposed actions which involve lying, raising, leaning, etc. However, in those processes involved in penetrative sex, it is the male partner who is most active:

He (Agent) enters (action) you (object)

This accords with the findings of other analysts that males are shown to act upon passive females in representations of sexual encounters.

You may like to compare the representation of sex in Text: 'Mind the leather', an extract from *Men's Health*. You will have noticed that the points made in relation to transitivity are echoed in this text, e.g. 'Enter your beloved from behind.' Another aspect which the texts have in common is the taken for granted assumption that in sexual encounters one's partner is of the opposite sex:

> He lies between your legs. . . . (*More!*)
> She kneels on the second step. . . . (*Men's Health*)

The privileging of heterosexuality as the norm is widespread in texts relating to sexual acts.

Incidentally, have you noticed how many everyday expressions contain sexual innuendos? Earlier in this unit it was stated 'the reader must *insert* themselves into the text'. We might also say someone asked *penetrating* questions. If someone has been deceived they might be described as having been *screwed*. Words associated with sex provide easy material for the comedian's double entendre.

Summary

This unit has attempted to explore some quite complex and perhaps emotive issues, especially in relation to sexuality which is generally thought of as being fixed and assigned at birth. For some time now it has generally been accepted that society has a hand in the construction of femininity and masculinity, but similar theories concerning sexuality are still being widely debated. This unit has merely suggested to readers that an examination of the text producer's choices in relation to transitivity often show that women are, as a matter of 'common sense', presented as passive, the *natural* opposite to men's activity.

index of terms

This is a form of combined glossary and index. Listed below are some of the key terms used in the book, together with brief definitions for purposes of reference. The page references will normally take you to the first use of the term in the book, where it will be usually shown in **bold**. In some cases, however, understanding of the term can be helped by exploring its uses in more than one place in the book, and accordingly more than one page reference is given.

amelioration 6
> A process by which a word acquires increasingly positive meanings; for example, words such as 'lord' and 'master'.

coherence 57
> A sentence or text is coherent when the ideas it contains make consistent sense to the hearer/ reader.

cohesion 84–8
> The patterns of language created within a text, mainly within and across sentence boundaries and which collectively make up the organisation of larger units of the text such as paragraphs. Cohesion can be both lexical and grammatical. Lexical cohesion is established by means of chains of words of related meaning linking across sentences; grammatical cohesion is established mainly by grammatical words such as 'the', 'this', 'it' and so on.

common sense 72
> The taken-for-granted beliefs which a society holds.

compound 13
> A word formed from two existing words.

conjunction 88
> A general term which describes words which link sentences and clauses together, indicating temporal, spatial, logical and causal relationships. Words such as 'and' and 'but' are **co-ordinating** conjunctions. **Subordinating** conjunctions are words such as 'when', 'where', 'which'. These join subordinate clauses to a main clause or to other subordinate clauses.

connotation 2
> The connotations of a word or concept are the associations it creates. For example, the connotations of December, mainly within British and North American culture, would be of 'cold', 'dark nights' and 'Christmas parties'. Connotations are often either individual or cultural.

contractions 23
> The shortening of a word or group of words usually indicated by an apostrophe e.g. 'I can't' instead of 'I cannot'.

determiner 16

This decides whether the noun is definite (the) or indefinite (a). Words such as 'all' and 'many' are determiners.

discourse 81–2

A term used in linguistics to describe the rules and conventions underlying the use of language in extended stretches of text, spoken and written. (Such an academic study is referred to as 'discourse analysis'.) The term is also used as a convenient general term to refer to language in action and the patterns which characterise particular types of language in action; for example, the 'discourse' of magazines.

ellipsis or elision 16

Ellipsis refers to the omission of part of a structure. It is normally used for reasons of economy and, in spoken discourse, can create a sense of informality.

etymology 82

The history of a word's source and development.

euphemism 73

A way of avoiding causing offence when referring to society's taboos. Euphemisms are polite, indirect expressions, e.g. 'down below' to mean genitalia.

genre xi

Another word for text-type. Examples of genre are report, review, essay.

heterogeneity 2

Composed of unrelated parts, or composed of elements which are not of the same type.

ideology 66, 82, 91

A body of ideas which reflect the beliefs of society.

idiomatic phrases 23

A sequence of words which function as a single unit of meaning and which cannot normally be interpreted literally e.g. 'going hell for leather', to produce the sense 'quickly'.

inferencing 72

Deducing a message from a statement when the message is not explicitly given.

intertextuality 73, 92

The way in which one text echoes or refers to another text. For example, an advertisement which stated 'To be in Florida in winter or not to be in Florida in winter' would contain an intertextual reference to a key speech in Shakespeare's *Hamlet*.

linguistic determinism 82

The idea that language influences a person's concept of reality.

modality 70

A general term which describes unrealised states and possible conditions and the forms of language which encode them such as 'possibly', 'perhaps', 'could be', 'ought to be'

modification: 15–16
pre-modification
Words appearing before the noun, mainly adjectives or adjective-like words.
Post-modification
Words appearing after the noun.

113

further reading

There aren't any books which deal specifically with the language of magazines, but there are several useful texts from a range of sources:

A book which looks at women's magazines from a historical perspective is:
Beetham, M. (1996) *A Magazine of Her Own?*, London: Routledge.

If you are interested in first person narratives:
Caldas Coulthard, C. (1996) 'Women who pay for sex and enjoy it, in C.R. Caldas-Coulthard and M. Coulthard (eds), *Texts and Practices*, London: Routledge.

A good follow-up to the work on ideology:
Fairclough, N. (1989) *Language and Power*, Harlow: Longman.

For an analysis of reader-responses to magazines:
Hermes, J. (1995) *Reading Women's Magazines: An Analysis of Everyday Media Use*, Cambridge: Polity Press.

For investigating images:
Kress, G. and VanLeewen, T. (1996) *Reading Images*, London: Routledge.

If you want to explore further the notion of the text 'population':
Talbot, M. (1992) 'The Construction of gender in a teenage magazine', in N. Fairclough (ed.), *Critical Language Awareness*, Harlow: Longman.

On consumerism and femininity:
Talbot, M. (1998) *Language and Gender: An Introduction*, Cambridge: Polity.

Pioneering texts on women's magazines are:
White, C. (1970) *Women's Magazines 1693–1968*, London: Michael Joseph.
Winship, J. (1987) *Inside Women's Magazines*, London: Pandora.

references

Brown, G. and Yule, G. (1983) *Discourse Analysis*. Cambridge: Cambridge University Press.

Carter, R. and Nash, W. (1990) *Seeing Through Language*. Blackwell.

Carter, R., Goddard, A., Reah, D., Sanger, K. and Bowring, M. (1997) *Working with Texts A core book for language analysis*. Routledge.

Fairclough, N. (1989) *Language and Power*, Harlow: Longman.

Fairclough, N. (1991) *Discourse and Social Change*. Polity.

Frazer, E. (1997) 'Teenage girls reading Jackie', in H. Baehr and A. Gray (eds), *Turning it on A reader in Women and Media*. Arnold.

Goddard, A. (1998) *The Language of Advertising*. Routledge.

Gough, V. and Talbot, M. (1996) 'Guilt over games boys play: coherence as a focus for examining the constitution of heterosexual subjectivity', in C.R. Caldas-Coulthard and M. Coulthard (eds) *Texts and Practices*. Routledge.

Halliday, M.A.K. (1985) *An Introduction to Functional Grammar*. Edward Arnold.

Kress, G. and VanLeeuwen, T. (1996) *Reading Images*. Routledge.

Lakoff, R. (1975) *Language and Woman's Place*. Harper and Row.

McCracken, E. (1996) 'The cover: window to the future self' *Turning it on A reader in Women and Media* (from *Decoding women's magazines from Mademoiselle to Ms.* Macmillan 1993).

Mills, S. (1995) *Feminist Stylistics*. Routledge.

Mills, S. (1997) *Discourse*. Routledge.

Schultz, M. (1975) 'The semantic derogation of women' in B. Thorne and N. Henley (eds), *Language and Sex: Difference and Dominance*. Rowley, MA, Newbury House.

Strinati, D. and Wagg, S. (eds) (1987) *Come on down? Popular Media, Culture and Post-War Britain*. Routledge.

Talbot, M. (1992) 'The construction of gender in a teenage magazine', in N. Fairclough (ed.), *Critical Language Awareness*. Longman.

Talbot, M. (1998) *Language and Gender An Introduction*. Polity.

Winship, J. (1992) *Inside Women's Magazines*. Pandora.